Praise for **AMBUSHED B**

"Michele Saffier and Allan Katz' *Ambushed by Betrayal* is an exceptionally well written and organized tour de force of describing the journey a betrayed partner takes from despair and confusion to hope and esteem in the recovery process. This book will quickly become an invaluable resource for anyone needing healing from the pain of betrayal."

~ **Kenneth M. Adams, Ph.D**. author of *Silently Seduced* and *When He's Married to Mom* and co-editor of *Clinical Management of Sex Addiction, 2ⁿᵈ edition.*

"If you are navigating the discovery of sexual addiction, *Ambushed by Betrayal* will be a priceless gift on your journey. Michele and Allan are compassionate, wise guides who walk you step-by-step through the healing process. Packed full of helpful coping strategies, relatable stories, and the finest clinical recovery wisdom, this workbook guides you gently through your healing process and helps you build a vision for a vibrant future."

~ **Jenna Riemersma, LPC, CSAT-S**, Clinical Director of the Atlanta Center for Relational Healing and bestselling author of *Altogether You: Discovering Personal and Spiritual Transformation with Internal Family Systems Therapy*

"When I read this wonderful workbook I thought about all the suffering people I know who I wished had immediate access to this very helpful tool! The authors are obviously experienced, very empathetic, and can really understand how betrayed partners feel and what they need to do to heal. This workbook can certainly enhance the healing process for partners who are working through their traumatic experiences, help them understand their vulnerabilities, and promote their undertaking the internal and external changes and decisions that will improve their lives. I highly recommend this book."

~ **Jennifer P Schneider, M.D.**
Author of *Back from Betrayal: Recovering from the Trauma of Infidelity*

"Michele Saffier and Allan J. Katz have written a practical guide to working through the trauma of partner betrayal. This step-by-step manual gives partners an opportunity to actively work through their feelings and emotions to take back the control they lost after sexual betrayal. This is an amazing teaching tool that will empower partners to gain their confidence they once lost. The authors are experts in the field of sex addiction and partner betrayal and have made it their mission to guide partners through the betrayal and into post-traumatic growth. The stories and quotes from partners are both inspiring and motivational. This book has it all!"

~ **Carol Juergensen Sheets**, ACSW, LCSW, CSAT, CCPS-C, PCC
Co-Author of *Help. Her. Heal. An Empathy Workbook for Sex Addicts to Help Their Partners Heal* & co-author of *Unleashing Your Power: Moving Through the Trauma of Partner Betrayal*

"In *Ambushed by Betrayal*, Michele Saffier and Allan Katz provide meaningful suggestions and exercises to help betrayed partners move forward into truth, healing, and restoration. What a fabulous accomplishment [by] Allan and Michele...a great addition to our work—much needed."

~ **Robert Weiss, PhD**, Chief Clinical Officer of Seeking Integrity and author of *Out of the Doghouse, Sex Addiction 101*, and *Prodependence*

On The Cover: *Kintsugi*

~

The Japanese art of Kintsugi is a perfect metaphor for the authors' approach to the process of healing for betrayed partners. In comparison with western culture where we embrace the perfect, the shiny, the new and the unbroken, in Japanese culture, objects have value and meaning that reaches far beyond their "intended" purpose. Vases have been passed down with purpose from ancestors. Serving dishes become a part of the family in the sense that they are present during important events in the life of a family. They hold a holy purpose—to serve. Western culture tends to discard broken objects or glue them back together in a way that hides the cracks—so no one notices—lest they judge the person for using or displaying a cracked object. The intention is to hide the cracks; to keep the breaks a "secret" because gluing broken things back together is seen as crude. In the eastern tradition, objects are valued. They are viewed as a part of the complex structure of family. When a pottery piece breaks, it is as if a member of the family has been harmed. Rather than hide the brokenness, Japanese culture believes they are to be honored, respected and valued. Rather than be embarrassed by the cracks, they are to be honored for the value they have in the family in the same way that elders are honored and valued for exactly who they are.

Broken pottery is mended with gold in order to honor and celebrate their brokenness. They are said to be more beautiful than their original form. Acknowledging, with visibility, that they are more valuable and stronger because of their repair. This process of mending is called *Kintsugi*; it treats breakage and repair as part of the history of an object, rather than something to disguise. As a philosophy, *Kintsugi* is similar to the Japanese philosophy of *wabi-sabi*, an embracing of the flawed or imperfect. Japanese aesthetics values marks of wear from the use of an object, highlighting the cracks and repairs as simply an event in the life of an object rather than allowing its service to end at the time of its damage or breakage.

Sooner or later we all carry scars—internal, external or both. We all break in different places and in different ways. *Kintsugi* celebrates the beauty of imperfection and acknowledges the strength and courage of repairing and highlighting adversity with gold. What a message of resilience, not just for pottery but for ourselves. There is real value in things that have been fixed, patched, and healed with the gold of experience, wisdom, and love. Betrayed partners are enriched, stronger, enduring, and wiser for their cracks.

AMBUSHED BY BETRAYAL

THE SURVIVAL GUIDE FOR BETRAYED PARTNERS ON THEIR HEROES' JOURNEY TO HEALTHY INTIMACY

Michele F. Saffier, LMFT, CSAT-S

with **Allan J. Katz**, LPC, CSAT

SANO PRESS, LLC
CLAREMONT, CA

SANO PRESS, LLC
CLAREMONT, CA

1st Edition

Cover spread, book design & layout by Chris Bordey.

Adobestock.com images in use with standard license. Shutterstock.com images in use with standard license. Additional images and graphics from Flaticon.com, Pixabay.com, and Unsplash.com in accordance with Creative Commons CC0 except where noted. All fonts in use with commercial license from Ultimatefontdownload.com, Fontesk.com, and system fonts. Sano Press feather trademark Sano Press, LLC.

ISBN–13: 978-1-956620-00-9

To Patt, whose capacity to be a source of strength and light, to offer love and hold faith in God when everything was taken from her, held her brokenness with grace and dignity, and who sought to make meaning out of her suffering. Her untimely death was the inspiration for this workbook, as recovering partners "show their work" to guide you who are beginning your heroes' journey today.

TABLE *of* CONTENTS

You have a problem, a life-changing, earth-shattering problem—your partner has cheated countless times. Your brain is spinning, and your emotions are all over the map. You feel embarrassed and alone, but you're not. This book wouldn't exist if there weren't others in your shoes. Now that you know there is a problem, you can take the steps you need to move forward in whatever capacity is best for you for now. The exercises in this chapter will help you begin the healing process and help you evaluate what is important to you as you move forward.

The "why" question is what betrayed partners find themselves coming back to over and over again. "Why did you engage in this behavior?" "Why did you lie...repeatedly?" Betrayed partners often feel that they can't move on and find closure without knowing the answer to the "why" question. The painful truth is that, for a person struggling with sex addiction, there is no good reason. It can be challenging for betrayed partners to hear and can take time to process fully. Though they may not understand the 'why?' behind the behavior, betrayed partners can gain answers that help provide clarity and make healing possible for themselves and the relationship.

At the root of addiction is trauma. Trauma is the problem, and sexual acting out is the solution—until the solution fails. And it always fails and results in more trauma. Deep wounds suffered young cause a level of pain that overwhelms the child. Because human beings are built to stay alive, the brain banishes the ordeal's worst feelings and memory. It locks them away **to keep the child alive**. Understanding the brain science of trauma and addiction enables the betrayed partner to see the big picture. Although the acting out had very little to do with the relationship or the partner, the consequences demolish both.

There are so many unanswered questions, and each question has ten questions behind it. Betrayers are reluctant to answer your questions because they fear the answers will cause you more harm. **Withholding information causes harm!** When the betrayer does break down and answer your questions, you will not get the whole story because they are still in denial. They are in denial of the fact that they are in denial. A therapist-led disclosure is the best way to get the information you need to make the most important decision of your life. If you choose to remain in your relationship, you must know what to expect in treatment and recovery.

In this chapter, your healing process begins. The exercises gently shift focus away from the betrayer and toward your tender and bruised heart. You will start to realize that time alone will not heal this wound and that suffering only gives rise to more suffering. It is essential **for your healing** to find your way through the pain, to prevent it from being unearthed at some later, unexpected time. All it takes is one cue in any given moment for an avalanche of pain to descend upon you. It is now time for you to release the all-encompassing anger. You learn to be the agent of your healing. Grief, sorrow, and despair will be faced, making way for the restoration of self.

As the pain recedes, the process of reconstruction begins. The exercises will guide you through a life review, revisiting memories—most all of which became tainted by your betrayer's choices. You will reflect on your relationship and decide which memories you will reclaim. Those that carry too much pain will be brought to closure so that they begin to soften back, taking up less space in your mind. Your life story begins to reconstruct, acknowledging two truths; (1) The events happened the way you have always remembered them, and (2) The deceit, dishonesty, and duplicity of the secret betrayal occurred as well. Your newfound wisdom helps you to see each situation differently.

"To err is human; to forgive, divine" ~Alexander Pope, 1711

Who is to be forgiven, your betrayer or you? The complexity of forgiveness and the consequences of unforgiveness are explored. Did you know that forgiveness of yourself is a sacred act? Unforgiveness and how it destroys trust in humanity will be understood. Through the exercises, you will face a choice that has **nothing** to do with your betrayer and **everything** to do with restoring you to wholeness and inner harmony.

This chapter endeavors to begin releasing the pain that has tainted precious memories. Grief, shame, anger, self-criticism, and self-hatred are just a few of the *emotions that need to be released, making way for hope, self-compassion, and tenderness to fill the space.*

Through this chapter's work, you will begin to feel like yourself again, albeit a wiser and sturdier version of yourself. You will rewrite your story and set about finding the meaning in your suffering. Although grittier and more authentic, you will move from victim to victor.

In the words of Alcoholics Anonymous, "It works if you work it." In other words, relationship healing depends on how hard each person works on their trauma and emotional recovery. Exercises in the chapter enable you to discern your wants, needs, boundaries, and deal-breakers, preparing you to co-construct an honest, vulnerable, and healthy relationship.

Those who have betrayed, lied and cheated share their experiences in the first few months after discovery. They have tremendous compassion for where you are right now and want you to know what was going through their minds when their cheating was discovered. They make no excuses. Their writing is honest and from the heart, sharing their raw experiences hoping that there may be a nugget to help you make it through the pain.

This chapter is for your betraying partner. Betrayed partners and the unfaithful offer their best suggestions for navigating the first three months and what is required to aid in your healing. Betrayed partners describe what they needed to survive the first year. The unfaithful are straightforward; they advise what **not** to do.

Acknowledgments

~

Michele F. Saffier, LMFT, CSAT-S

I am most grateful for the partners that have entrusted me with their tattered hearts; the brave men and women over the past twenty-five years who have courageously sought help; Tuesday night and Thursday night partners groups; and the many betrayed partners who sought healing in the daylong and weekend intensives. The bravery I witnessed while traveling alongside them on their sacred journey taught me about the capacity to transcend the most horrific pain, break completely apart and then to embody compassion, wisdom, and wholeness. They celebrate their brokenness. Their beauty and strength are heartening. Their courage is to be admired.

The seeds of this book have been germinating for over thirty years when I set out to understand myself. I discovered that vulnerable conversations with friends, reading self-help books, and working in therapy were meaningful but weren't enough to create fundamental change. The self-awareness and insight that I sought to create the life I wanted required a deeper dive inward. And so began my heroes' journey.

Through my love of learning, I attended seminars on mindful eating, breathwork, inner child work, voice dialogue, guided visualization, past-life regression, grief, and mourning retreats, sweat lodge, chanting, mindfulness-based stress reduction training, experiential intensives, Eye Movement Desensitization and Reprocessing, Internal Family Systems work, and even a plant-guided wisdom session.

The guides that I have met along the way have been integral to my personal growth. Allen Brooks, my wise guide and mentor these thirty-four years, taught me to meditate, shared my passion for spiritual enlightenment, and has always had my back. Eric Field showed me that the most vital tool I have as a therapist is me; my presence as a safe and compassionate guide allows clients to access their own inherent wisdom. I am grateful to Elaine Leader, Ph.D., for hiring me as a young therapist to teach teenagers how to help their peers in crisis at TEENLINE at Cedars-Sinai Medical Center, Rob Weiss, PhD., for teaching me how to work with people struggling with sex addiction, igniting my passion for aiding in healing traumatized by betrayal. And Richard Leedes, Ph.D., and Bunny Lawrence who taught me that betrayed partners are not "codependent," but rather, hurt deeply because they have loved deeply.

My heartfelt thanks to M.T. for her steady support and for continuing to gently push me along. To my cohort, Allan Katz, I offer my heartfelt thanks for helping my dream become a reality. And finally, I am grateful to Marilyn Mason for spear-heading the project, for her patience and support, her tenacity, and her extraordinary editor's eye. Marilyn, I couldn't have gotten over the finish line without you!

While writing this book has been a passion for me, it comes with great sacrifice. I have deep gratitude for my children, Bayley and Ethan. They loved and supported me unconditionally through periods of doubt, enthusiastic passion, endless requests to "run this by you," my frequent obsessing about the book, and my absence as mom and wise guide.

Finally, I am forever grateful to Steven, my husband and beloved, for supporting me as I followed my passions, for his unending willingness to listen to me, for believing in me at times that I did not, for his unwavering loyalty, and for walking the journey alongside me.

~ Michele

Allan J. Katz, LPC, CSAT

Several years ago, Michele and I met at a psychodrama training. A couple years later at an IITAP symposium, Michele asked me to help her write this book. She had compiled hundreds of actual client quotations about their experiences as betrayed spouses, and she wanted to write a book to help them heal from betrayal trauma.

Since I had written two books previously and had knowledge of working with publishers and self-publishing, she asked me to assist her in writing, editing, and marketing this book. After two years of writing, debating, and organizing, this work is finally complete. I want to acknowledge and thank Michele, my co-author, for this opportunity to add, edit, and contribute to her magnum opus of twenty-five years as a Marriage and Family Therapist and Certified Sex Addiction Therapist, among her many other certifications and accomplishments. Thank you from the bottom of my heart for all you do, have done, and continue to do for our field and for me personally.

I would also like to thank my wife, Esther, for her encouragement, love, and support in working on this workbook and in being my biggest fan in our lives together.

~ Allan

AMBUSHED BY BETRAYAL

"Mental health is an ongoing process of dedication to reality at all costs."

~ M. Scott Peck, *The Road Less Traveled*

INTRODUCTION

The road ahead may seem daunting at this moment. The possibility that you can ever feel whole again and that your spouse will become a person who lives with integrity may seem impossible now but, in my 25 years working with chronic infidelity, I can confidently state that I have witnessed remarkable transformations. I have witnessed miracles with couples that did not have even a thread of hope, or as former client Linda said, *"I don't have a grain of sand of hope,"* creating a deeper and more loving relationship than I could have ever imagined.

You are reading these pages because a part of you needs to deal with the crisis at hand and have your life back. There may also be a part of you that is resentful that you are even reading these pages and thinking "*This isn't my problem, he needs to fix himself.*" These may be two among many parts of you that have a whole host of feelings: shock, horror, confusion, sadness, and rage to name a few. After all, you didn't seek help and you certainly didn't ask for this problem. And, here you are. With trepidation, reluctance and, perhaps, resentment, you are beginning a process of healing. Those who choose this book are in the midst of a deep and unfamiliar crisis that is frightening. It is a crisis of mind, heart, and of soul. It is an existential crisis leaving many questioning the meaning of their life. The horrible discovery of your partners' deception has forced you into a darkness that can feel fatal, hopeless and never-ending.

Without your permission, you have been thrust into a profound journey. It is dark at times, for sure. It is through the darkness that you will find your light. You only need to do one thing—stay with the process no matter how bleak or hopeless. You only need to believe one thing: *You are worth taking the time to heal yourself.*

Your journey is a heroes' journey and, like Ulysses, Harry Potter, Frodo, Simba and Luke Skywalker, you will fight two-headed dragons, Harry Potter's Voldemort, Simba's Scar, Luke Skywalker's Death Star, and monsters of your own making. You will be challenged with emotional trials, obstacles, and tests. You will face the truths of your life. It will not be easy, but I promise, *if you stay on the journey and hang on for dear life, you will come through to the other side stronger, wiser, and whole.*

Chapter 1 is a front-line resource to help you to get through the first days and weeks after discovery of your betrayer's infidelity. Chapter 2 focuses on one of the greatest challenges of your healing—making sense of why your betrayer chose to deceive you and betray the sanctity of your relationship. Chapter 3 offers an understanding of the underpinnings of compulsive sexual behavior from the vantage point of compelling traumatic events of the past and their lifelong influence on a person throughout their life, the neuroscience of compulsive behavior, and other current issues that may lead to maladaptive ways of coping with stress. Chapter 4 offers direct help and guidance for formal disclosure—a therapist-guided process of learning the full extent of the betrayal.

Learning the full extent of your betrayer's actions forces you into facing the reality of your circumstance. This is the point where your healing journey begins. The chapters ahead focus on your heroes' journey of healing and strengthening your whole self.

Chapter 10 discusses the possibility of reconciliation. Chapter 11 offers information for you directly from people struggling with sex addiction. Finally, Chapter 12 offers information and advice from people in recovery from sex addiction *for your betrayer*.

ASSUMPTIONS

Before you begin your journey, it is important to acknowledge a few basic assumptions:

- You are doing the very best that you can in dealing with your emotions considering the catastrophic discovery of your beloved's cheating.

- You want to regulate your emotions.

- You want to heal.

- You want to overcome your trauma.

- You understand that, although you did not cause the situation that resulted in your trauma, you are responsible for your own healing.

- You realize that your usual methods for coping with stress are not effective under the current circumstances and you must learn new skills to manage this crisis.

TERMS/DEFINITIONS

Throughout the book, terms will be used interchangeably, regardless of gender in order to make the material easier to understand. The terms found throughout the book are in italics and include:

The betrayed: The innocent party. The partner that did not step away, or cheat, in the relationship. The partner who was harmed by the acting-out behavior. *Betrayed partner, the partner, the betrayed, the wounded partner, the offended partner, the trauma wounded partner.*

The betrayer: The one that caused harm. Refers to the behavior only and does not reflect judgement, negative bias, condemnation, or prognosis. *The unfaithful, the betrayer, the S.A. (the person struggling with sex addiction), the offending partner, the offender.*

Acting out: A behavior or action that is destructive to self or others. The term 'acting out' is commonly used in the addiction field. *Deception, infidelity, acting out.*

Betrayal trauma: A trauma that is perpetrated by someone with whom the victim is reliant upon for love, support, and survival. It is a violation of the relationship contract, or agreement, of fidelity and honesty. Betrayal trauma can be experienced by a caregiver or close relative, an institution (school, job), military, law enforcement, healthcare system, or a therapist. *The betrayed, betrayed partner.*

Affair partner: An acting out partner, or third party: The other person who has engaged in secret behavior with the betrayer.

Hero: The term originates in greek mythology. Hero was a priestess of Aphrodite.

Heroes' journey: Joseph Campbell, a professor at Sarah Lawrence College who was an expert in literature, said "A hero is someone who has given his or her life to something bigger than oneself." He stated that anyone can become a hero—on purpose or even accidentally. But it involves a painful evolution that is a prerequisite to greatness. On the journey, the hero is tested, meets allies and enemies, and prepares for an ordeal that will truly test their mettle. The ordeal forces the hero to face their worst fears. When they survive their journey, they gain valuable knowledge and insight that transforms the hero. Finally, the reborn hero shares what they've learned on their journey with others.

The heroes' journey elevates your trauma healing to a distinguished and noble level. Surviving your betrayal trauma may not seem heroic but, if you stay with the process, you will grow as a result of your trials and you will become wise, dignified, and enlightened.

The path of your heroes' journey is shaped by all of those who have come before you. They have slayed their dragons, conquered their fears and gained wisdom that they are passing on to you in the pages of this workbook. Throughout the book, you will learn how to reduce your fears, hurt, and anger. With the help of exercises, you will delve deeply within and take control of your own healing. You will be encouraged to engage all of your senses, *all of* **you**, to survive the nightmare you are living through and then to build a strong, wise and autonomous self.

Partners overwhelmingly urged me to remind the reader to remember to breathe throughout the chapters. Several partners were so disoriented the first month that they didn't realize they unconsciously held their breath. Linda said that she actually forgot how to breathe. Use the workbook as your survival guide.

An essential first step to any journey is to have what you will need on hand. In preparation for your heroes' journey, take time now to put together your toolkit.

UNHELPFUL THOUGHT BOX

Items needed and directions to make your unhelpful thought box.

- Medium-sized box.

- X-Acto blade.

- Art supplies.

- Thick black sharpie.

- Pad of paper.

- Pen.

Directions: Cut a slit in the lid of the box big enough to slide a piece of paper through. Decorate and embellish it. Tap into your creative energy and use this as an opportunity for healing through the creative process. Write the name of the box using the black sharpie. Put it in a prominent place. You will be using it frequently.

Purpose: A place where uncomfortable memories, feelings, and thoughts can be stored safely.

When a negative, discouraging, or anger-provoking thought comes up, write it down and put it in the box. This action often breaks the pattern of obsessive thinking which causes negative feelings, sending you into the pit of pain.

EMERGENCY OR SOOTHE BOX

When we are very distressed, it is difficult to think rationally and to decide how to help ourselves. We can, therefore, resort to using self-destructive behaviors which may help at that moment, but can cause other problems later and in the long-term. It can be useful to keep an "emergency" or "soothe" bag or box, in a prominent and handy place, so that when you feel overwhelmingly distressed, you can go to your bag or box and find something that will help you cope and/or feel better.

Make your emergency or soothe box[1] and fill it with meaningful and helpful objects or reminders. Include an object for each of your senses. For example, a photo is visual, music or an instrument are hearing, essential oils represent smell, gum or a mint represent taste, and a silky scarf or woolly socks represent touch. We feel our feelings in our bodies. Stimulating our senses can be soothing and calming. Use any bag or box or other container, and decorate it as you wish.

AFFIRMATIONS

Throughout the book, writing prompts will help you to navigate your darkest times. Respond to the prompts as you are reading, if possible. The AFFIRMATIONS worksheet in the appendix offers many possibilities for keeping negative thoughts in check. Choose those that fit.

A GRATITUDE JOURNAL

Write one gratitude each day. Examples of gratitudes are I *am grateful for my health and I am grateful that I have time to enjoy my cup of coffee this morning.*

A PERSONAL JOURNAL

Partners overwhelmingly recommend that you have a journal to record your thoughts and feelings, as well as for art, poetry, pictures or any other form of self-expression. Additionally, although the workbook provides space to respond to questions, don't limit your responses to the space on the page. If you need more space, use your personal journal.

---

[1](http://www.get.gg)

PERSONAL OBJECTS

- A palm stone or any object that you can hold in your hand to help you to relax.

- A candle, scented essential oils or any other scent or aroma that soothes.

- A religious or spiritual item that provides comfort.

- A stuffed animal. Don't underestimate the comfort of a stuffed animal!

Above all else, **faith in yourself and in your capacity to heal even in the midst of the storm.**

A NOTE ABOUT EXERCISES

Throughout this workbook, one of three characters will appear next to the word **"EXERCISE"**: the *Wise Owl*, the *Magnolia Tree*, or the *Enlightened Sun*. Each character identifies the level of intensity of the exercise. Complete the *Wise Owl* exercises on your own. The *Magnolia Tree* exercises are likely to bring up painful emotions and require more time and deep thought. Consider working on the *Magnolia Tree* exercises with the help of a friend or sponsor/mentor. The *Enlightened Sun* exercises and more intense writings should be worked on with your therapist. These are simply suggestions to help you along your own personal heroes' journey.

 The **Wise Owl** represents those exercises to do on your own.

 The **Magnolia Tree** represents those exercises you might do with a friend, mentor, or sponsor.

 The **Enlightened Sun** represents those intense exercises you should do with your therapist.

Through the Gateway

by Eva Pierakos

Through the gateway of feeling your weakness lies your strength;

through the gateway of feeling your pain lies your pleasure and joy;

through the gateway of feeling your fear lies your security and safety;

through the gateway of feeling your loneliness lies your capacity to have fulfillment, love and companionship;

through the gateway of feeling your hate lies your capacity to love;

through the gateway of feeling your hopelessness lies true and justified hope;

through the gateway of accepting the lacks of your childhood lies your fulfillment now.

Through the Gateway from Pathwork Lecture 190. Reprinted with permission from the Pathwork® Foundation

CHAPTER 1

THE PROBLEM: SOMETHING TERRIBLE HAS HAPPENED!

I t's as if you've been pushed out of a plane and you are falling, falling, falling with no parachute. You feel detached, disconnected, far away. You feel like everything is muted, as though you are experiencing the world under water.

Everything is upside down. Your world is broken to pieces, fragmented. You can't tell anyone, or you can't stop telling everyone. You feel overwhelming shame, thinking "How stupid am I?" "I'm such a fool!" "I'm an idiot!" "I'm so gullible!"

You worry that you are mentally ill, that you are crazy.

You are not crazy! There is nothing wrong with you!

This is probably the most shocking and confounding crisis you have ever experienced. Most partners say discovering their beloved betrayed them is by far the worst crisis of their life. How can you possibly wrap your head around what you saw or heard? How can this possibly be true? After all, you know him and never thought he would cheat. This rocks the very foundation of the values you both believed and lived within. What is most disturbing is that you were going about your daily routine *in the safety of your own home* and, in an instant, a discovery upends your world. It happens through a knock at the door, an unexpected text, the ring of the telephone or the most common form of discovery—turning on the computer to check email.

In the first moment and the first hour and the first day, the shock is so profound that it is hard to comprehend. It feels as though it can't be happening and that it is surreal. It feels as if you are suddenly outside of yourself watching a movie, watching yourself react and not feeling connected to your own body. International Trauma Expert, Dr. Peter Levine states that when we are in a situation that *our brain* experiences as frightening, we automatically go into a freeze response. We are thrust into a primal survival strategy, commonly referred to as being like a "deer in the headlights." It is the state of being "beside yourself." Partners describe it as being frozen, numb, like being in an altered state. Being lied to in such a profound manner by your partner, lover, sweetheart, beloved is abnormal and unprecedented. *Even if you have suspected or discovered a lie or inexplicable situation in the past, what is happening to you now is unparalleled.*

STOP FOR A MOMENT & BREATHE.

EXERCISE: What is Your Story?

Take a few minutes to describe how you learned about your partner cheating on you. This may be the first time that you are putting into words what happened to you. It is excruciating to relive the situation, but it's an essential part of your healing. The more you write about your traumatic event—the worst moment—the less pain it will cause over time *because you will become less reactive, or upset, by the event.*

WHAT DO I DO FIRST?

You can expect to feel agitated, overwhelmed, and afraid. You will likely have difficulty concentrating—feeling like you are in a fog. It is hard to know what to do first. The immediate need is for safety, structure and boundaries. The 5 areas to attend to first are:

- Safety—physical and emotional

  - Are you worried about physical violence including holes punched in a wall, throwing objects, pushing, physical intimidation including bumping his chest against you in a threatening manner?

  - Are you experiencing emotional harm, for example: gaslighting, yelling, screaming in your face, name calling ("You're such a..."), emotional withdrawal, or silent treatment, stonewalling, being told how to think or feel, threats of harm to reputation, finances, child custody ("If you tell anyone..." or "If you divorce me...")?

- Financial

  - Do you have access to joint assets, or money, for immediate needs (gas, food, etc.)?

  - If the discovery includes significant monies spent on acting out, contact financial institutions to prevent further loss of monies.

- Nourishment

  - Do you have enough access to basic needs including food, water, and shelter?

- Medical

  - If you regularly take medication, be sure to take it as prescribed.

  - If the discovery involves sex outside the relationship, schedule an appointment with your physician to discuss possible sexually-transmitted diseases.

  - If you are experiencing medical symptoms of stress including migraines, ongoing stomach upset, diarrhea, panic attacks, or any other physical pain contact your physician.

- Emotional support

  - Do you have one trusted friend or family member in whom you can confide?

  - Be sure that you can trust that whomever you confide in will maintain complete confidentiality and will not judge or pressure you to make a decision ("If it were me, I'd throw him out").

The question most frequently asked by partners is, *"How can I live with my betrayer after what I have learned? Should he move out? Should I kick him out of the bedroom?"* You are faced with decisions at a time when it is hard to remember to brush your teeth. You likely feel disgusted, repulsed, sympathetic, afraid all at once. Although the intensity of these feelings will subside over the next month, *it is important that you consider your emotional and physical safety first.*

If you feel emotionally safe with your betrayer at home *right now*, you may want him to sleep in another room for the time being. If you do not feel emotionally safe, you may want him to sleep at a friend's or family member's home, or a hotel. You may change your mind several times on the same day. Although this may seem to be "irrational" behavior, what you are thinking or feeling is completely normal. Remember that this is an unprecedented situation. Before going further, assess your immediate situation with the ensuring safety exercise. Brace yourself. You are facing difficult questions. Mental health requires fully facing the situation with your head up and eyes open.

BREATH BREAKS

Throughout this book you will see breath break boxes. Practice self-care, take a break when you remember to *and practice the breath breaks often.* Practicing breath breaks will help you manage the intense overwhelming emotions and will become an important tool in your trauma healing toolkit.

Mindfulness Breath Break

~

Stop. Place your hand on your stomach—the area above your belly button and below your diaphragm. Keep your shoulders still. Inhale a long and slow breath in *through your nose*, feeling your hand move out. The breath will pull your diaphragm down and push your belly out. Feel your hand move out with your belly. Exhale *through your mouth* slowly. Feel your belly and your hand move in.

ENSURING SAFETY

Responding to the following questions will help you to discern what you need right now. Expect that your basic safety needs will change. Focus on today.

1.   What do I need to feel physically and emotionally safe?

   _____

2.   Is there physical violence present in my home today?

   _____

3.   Is there verbal abuse, or speaking in a demeaning, aggressive, argumentative, belittling or mocking tone, begging for or demanding forgiveness, harassment ("Why did you do that; that is so stupid), demands to talk about the crisis even though you have said "no," following you in a threatening manner, threats of dire consequences?

   _____

4.   Fiduciary abuse: Does your betrayer control your spending, including: scrutinizing your expenses, grocery bills, vacation planning, not allowing you to work, assets in betrayer's name only, etc.?

   _____

When there is physical or verbal abuse, the safest first step is for you (and your children) to leave the home.

5.   Has unprotected sexual contact occurred?

   _____

6.   Do I need to make an appointment with my doctor to have STD testing?

   _____

7. Do I have access to joint monies (savings, retirement accounts)?

    _____

8. How much money has been spent without my permission?

    _____

9. If my betrayer has admitted to spending joint monies "acting out," do I need to secure my finances?

    _____

FOLLOWING IS A GUIDE TO SECURING FINANCES:

- Secure access to all bank accounts, account numbers and passwords including:

  - Bank statements for the past year from each account

  - Access and statements to retirement accounts

  - Access to safe deposit boxes and home safe

What do you need to do to secure your finances? Is your access to money restricted? Do you need your own money? If so, purchasing American Express or Visa cards during grocery shopping allows you to have access to money. Is it safe to withdraw money from joint bank accounts?

List any action that needs to be taken immediately:

Safety: _____

Financial: _____

Medical: _____

In order to manage through extreme circumstances, it is helpful to identify exactly what you *need*, rather than what you may want. Webster's Dictionary defines a need as "a physiological or psychological requirement for the well-being of an organism" and a want is defined as "a desire." As you continue through this process, your needs will change and it will be important to identify *those* needs. Following is a list of basic personal needs.

 EXERCISE: Immediate Needs

Identify your immediate needs by circling your 5 most important needs right now. Put a check mark next to the needs that are a challenge today.

Food, Water, Clothing, Shelter	To feel at ease
Health	Vulnerability
Sleep	Respect
Financial Security	Self-respect
Income	Competence
Trust	Strength
Fidelity	Friends
Loyalty	Community
Affection	Intimacy

Acceptance	Help
Support	Tolerance
To be heard/listened to	Kindness
Love	Consideration
Courtesy	Compassion
Nurturing	Humility
Accountability	Trustworthy confidant

EMERGENCY TOOLS AND STRATEGIES TO GET THROUGH A CRISIS

Use these tools when you are in an emotional crisis:

1. Look for circles—look around you and notice circles: a coffee cup, bowl, coffee can, etc.

2. Taming runaway thoughts—tell yourself "The worst is over. It's not happening now."

3. Write thoughts and feelings down and put them in your Unhelpful Thought Box.

4. Listen for sounds around you: birds, barking, music, dishwasher, traffic.

5. Put your palms together and rub vigorously, feel the friction. Feel the vibration in your hands when you stop.

6. Move your body—pace, shake your body, flail your arms, stomp your feet, stretch, dance, jump up and down.

7. Breathe in through the nose, hold for four counts and out through your mouth for eight counts.

8. Take your shoes off and rub the bottoms of your feet on the floor.

9. Use 5,4,3,2,1: Name five things you see, four things you can hear, three things you can touch (touch them now), two things you can smell and one slow, deep breath.

10. Read something aloud.

DAILY SELF-CARE

Begin a daily practice of listing:

- Something you have gratitude for today.

  - *I am grateful for my dog today.*

- A current challenge that you are experiencing.

  - *I am having a hard time being around my betrayer's family because they don't know my secret.*

- One positive affirmation about yourself.

  - *I have compassion for myself.*

THE POWER OF ANALOGIES

Throughout the book you will find analogies. Analogies are extremely powerful. They enable us to make sense of a novel situation. They allow us to integrate something we can't understand. This allows us to make sense of an abnormal circumstance. The analogies throughout the book will help you build your own framework so you can make sense of all that you are coping with today.

What you are experiencing is a Tsunami, a 10.0 magnitude earthquake, a bomb dropped on your home, your own 9/11. It's as if your life as you knew it was stolen along with your most cherished memories. How to think? How to sleep? Eat? Breathe? You don't know what to do next. You have lost all sense of time. Your heart hurts. Your soul hurts. You are lost.

PAUSE FOR A MOMENT & BREATHE.

EXERCISE: The Power of Analogies

What analogy describes your situation today? Refer to ANALOGIES in the appendix for suggestions.

_____

_____

_____

_____

YOU ARE TRAUMATIZED!

You have suffered the worst and most traumatizing circumstance imaginable. You were abused, tricked, and lied to by the one person in the world you trusted the most and who was supposed to have your back. The one you adored and pledged to love, honor, and cherish until death do you part—your beloved—now your perpetrator. Suddenly you are feeling utterly unsafe in your safe haven, your own home. Worse, the crime was committed over and over and over again. Your beloved cheated with countless others and then kissed you good night and fell asleep effortlessly. You realize that this obsession with pornography replaced you. He preferred young, perfect, seductive women on a screen while masturbating. "They" became his wife. You are heartbroken when you realize you were there all along, yearning for sexual intimacy—but he chose "them."

You can't be around people. You can't handle surprises. Noises startle you. You are in the grocery store and, seemingly out of nowhere, you become overwhelmed with anxiety and a sudden urge to flee the store. You begin to realize that you easily become anxious and fearful in unfamiliar situations. Randomly, something that you experience leaves you overwhelmed, afraid and confused.

You find that you are triggered by anything, everything, or nothing. People, songs, television, books, the computer, your cell phone, malls, concerts, family, restaurants—anything can suddenly become a cause of distress that may keep you in bed for the rest of the day. You are *not* codependent. You were *not* given this burden by your higher power as your cross to bear. It is *not* your mission to heal your betrayer, the one who caused you suffering.

DO NOT ALLOW ANYONE—YOUR PARTNER, YOUR THERAPIST, A BLOG POST— ANYONE—TELL YOU THAT:

- You're too sensitive.

- You are blowing "things" out of proportion.

- The behaviors are "normal."

- All men watch porn.

- All women flirt.

- You are frigid.

- It's stress relief.

- What do you expect when you don't have enough sex?

- It's "normal" in business to take clients to strip clubs when entertaining.

- You knew something was wrong but you stuck your head in the sand.

- We are ALL addicted to cell phones.

- So what if he takes his cell phone to the bathroom!

PAUSE...BREATHE.

MY BEST ADVICE FOR ALL WHO WALK THE PATH BEHIND ME...

"The shock was so intense. I devoured everything I could get my hands on to make sense of what was happening. I was so anxious that there were times that I actually forgot to breathe! My contribution to the book is to remind you to breathe."

~ Alicia, *warrior woman*

The way in which we draw a breath influences our physical and mental health. Oxygen keeps our blood flowing, our organs and tissues healthy, and impacts our thinking brain. A recent study shows a direct link between shallow breathing and judgement, memory, and a decreased ability to recognize fearful stimuli.[2] Breathing in through the nose is called diaphragm breathing. Diaphragm breathing expands the lungs, pushes the diaphragm down and stomach out fully oxygenating the system. Breathing in through the mouth, is called shallow breathing. When taking a shallow breath, the shoulders rise and the breath remains in the chest. Shallow breathing increases carbon dioxide in the system, increases anxiety, and can cause a panic attack. This type of breathing can quickly become a negative, repetitive habit. Shallow breathing causes stress and stress causes shallow breathing.

Partners often report that they notice they unconsciously hold their breath—as if waiting for another trauma. They also report that they feel like they can't take a deep breath and are afraid they are having a heart attack. When they learn diaphragm breathing, partners report less anxiety, brain fog, forgetfulness, fear thoughts, and they don't startle as easily. Throughout the book you will be reminded to breathe. Although you are feeling deep pain, be gentle with yourself and take time to pause, renew, and to breathe. These breaks provide you with the opportunity to center and better understand the information provided.

[2]http://jneurosci.org/content/36/49/12448

WHEN STRESSED, IT'S HARD TO REMEMBER HOW TO BREATHE!

Breath Break

~

Take a moment to close your eyes, inhale for four counts, taking the breath all the way down to your diaphragm and then exhaling for eight counts out your mouth. Repeat 5 times. Open your eyes and notice the sensation of calm inside.

I USED TO BE A CONFIDENT WOMAN...

"Prior to discovery of my husband's emotional affairs ("we are just friends") and that he had sex with many, many women throughout our marriage, I was a confident woman. I did important work in the world. I was capable, competent. I was a multi-tasker. I looked forward to each day, jumping out of bed and excited for what lay ahead. After discovery, I was racked with anxiety, fearful of the day, unsure of what shoe would drop next. I pulled the covers over my head and stayed in bed. I became hopeless, depressed, inconsolable. I suddenly questioned myself and my judgement, after all—how capable was I if I didn't see the signs of my husband's behavior?—and I now realize there were many.

"As for my husband, before discovery he was an anxious, negative person. He was easily rattled. He would often come home from work obsessing about something that happened, frustrated that his colleagues were idiots not *committed to their jobs. He was unsure of himself, doubted his competency and needed guidance to handle even the smallest problems at work. I was his cheerleader, his business coach and his doting wife. After his last affair partner (there were many over our 30 years of marriage) called me and told me every sordid detail of my husband's behavior and I confronted him, something bizarre happened next... He was relieved and said he had never felt better in his whole life! He said he felt liberated now that the secret was out. He slept better than he had in years and he looked better than he ever had. In that moment it was as if a truckload of manure, **his** manure, was removed from his shoulders and then dumped on me and buried me."*

~ Janice, *betrayed spouse*

BETRAYAL TRAUMA

What this partner describes is a unique phenomenon to the kind of trauma you are in the midst of, *betrayal trauma*. Patrick Carnes, Ph.D. the "founding father" of sex addiction treatment, aptly named his first book (the first to identify compulsive sexual behavior as addictive) *Out of The Shadows* because upon discovery, the betrayer emerges out of the shadows and into the light of day. In the light of day and with the secret exposed, the betrayer's shame and guilt decreases significantly. After all, the person struggling with addiction's worst fears didn't materialize—the fears that kept the behavior secret. The problem is that now you are at risk of taking on his shame and making it your own. For your emotional health and wellness, you must fight to prevent that possibility. The following chart illustrates the experience of the couple after discovery.

BETRAYER'S REALITY	BETRAYED PARTNER'S REALITY
Finally, I feel connected!	I feel so alone.
I can finally breathe.	Sometimes I feel like I've forgotten how to breathe.
I am reclaiming my integrity.	I've been betrayed and lied to.
I've never loved my partner more.	I've never felt so unloved and unworthy.
Finally, I am honest.	I must keep the secret. I am now lying.
The weight of the world is on my shoulders!	I feel burdened with his secret.
My lifelong belief that I am not good enough, lovable or worthy are dissipating!	I've lost my confidence and self-esteem. What would my friends and family think of me if they knew?
I feel connected, plugged in. I finally feel connected to people.	I can't face anyone. I can't pretend to be happy so I've stopped seeing friends & family.

It is important to know that there is no one "right" way to handle this situation. This is a profound, abnormal, inexplicable, and life-altering trauma. There may have been discoveries or even admissions in the past, help sought, healing felt, sincere apologies extended and an agreement to move ahead. It is perfectly reasonable that you believed and trusted your partner. Ordinarily when someone is confronted with bad behavior and they apologize and promise that it won't happen again, it doesn't.

PAUSE FOR A MOMENT AND BREATHE

EXERCISE: Clarity of Thought

This exercise can help you to sort out your thoughts and feelings related to where you are right now.

Begin gently. Sit in a comfortable chair with a pen and notebook. Prepare a cup of tea, take a breath break and then respond to the questions below. This work is not easy. Expect that you will feel sad, defeated, hopeless, bereft. And you will likely feel angry, offended, disgusted, ashamed, and even horrified. Keep in mind that the exercises are intended to help you to "lean in" to your circumstance; to identify and understand intense feelings and thoughts. *You can't heal what you can't feel.*

How have you been feeling since discovery?

_____

_____

_____

How do you feel toward yourself since discovery?

_____

_____

_____

What are the negative judgements you have about yourself since discovery?

_____

_____

What are beliefs you have about yourself since discovery?

List the thoughts that won't stop running through your mind since discovery:

About you:

About your relationship:

About your past in your marriage:

About the future:

_____

_____

_____

Where do I want to be by the end of this workbook?

How would I like to feel about myself?

_____

_____

_____

What do I want to think about myself?

_____

_____

_____

How would I like to feel about my relationship?

_____

_____

_____

What do I want to think about my relationship?

How would I like to feel about my betrayer?

What would I like to think about my betrayer?

Use a pencil for this next section. You may change your answers many times during this process. List 3 things that you need to help you become able to choose what you want to think and feel by the end of the book:

1.

2.

3.

PAUSE...BREATHE.

Reread your list of 3 things you need to help yourself heal. If your betrayer is on the list, cross him off. Your betrayer is not capable of giving you what you need *at this time.* He is in crisis, albeit a crisis of his own making, and is unable to provide the much-needed empathy that you are entitled to and that you deserve. He may be insisting that he understands what you are going through and that he is there for you—with complete sincerity and humility—but he is in the earliest stages of facing the magnitude of the harm he caused. Because he didn't go through it, he is unable to *feel* empathy. He can try to offer sympathy, though. Guilt, shame, self-hatred, and the sudden realization that he could lose everything will override his best efforts to listen, comfort and offer empathy.

Before moving on, be sure your list of 3 things you need to heal *are indeed 3 things that will help you heal!* If not, rewrite the list. This is an essential list for you as it will be your guidepost along your journey.

1. _____

2. _____

3. _____

The exercise probably brought up painful feelings. We welcome all feelings. There is no benefit in trying to avoid feelings. They will pop back up when you least expect it, traumatizing you all over again. It is important to keep your head and your body connected. Betrayed partners can't stop thinking of "worst case scenarios," which cause shallow breathing, increased stress and anxiety, keeping you forever looping disturbing scenes in your head. Because feelings are felt in the body, partners often say that they feel disconnected from themselves. In order to break the endless loop, practice checking in with your body daily. It is a guaranteed stress reducer.

Learning to identify what we feel and where in our bodies we feel it enables us to reduce stress and distress. When you are stressed, take a moment and find the place in your body where you are feeling some kind of energy, for example: tingling, tightness, fluttering, pain. Then, using the SUD's scale, rate the level of distress. Finally, do the feeling breath exercise.

 EXERCISE: Subjective Unit of Distress Scale (SUDS SCALE)

Rate how you are feeling at this moment on a scale of 1–10

1	2	3	4	5	6	7	8	9	10

Peaceful   *Uncomfortable*   *Worst I've ever felt*

← A C T I O N ←   → R E A C T I O N →

Using the SUDS scale, rate how you are feeling right now with regard to the feelings listed below.

	Peaceful			*Uncomfortable*				*Worst I've ever felt*		
FEAR	1	2	3	4	5	6	7	8	9	10
ANGER	1	2	3	4	5	6	7	8	9	10
RAGE	1	2	3	4	5	6	7	8	9	10
HOPELESSNESS	1	2	3	4	5	6	7	8	9	10
DISCOURAGEMENT	1	2	3	4	5	6	7	8	9	10
DESPONDENCY	1	2	3	4	5	6	7	8	9	10
ADD YOUR OWN FEELING: _____	1	2	3	4	5	6	7	8	9	10

The feeling I am having the most trouble with is: _____

The coping strategy I will use is: _____

_____

Feeling Check

~

Sitting in a comfortable position, close your eyes. Focus on feeling your breathing. Feel the air entering in through your nose, filling up your lungs and blowing out of your mouth. Inhale slowly through your nose. Focus your attention on the place in your body where you feel energy. Breathe out of your mouth and *through* that place in your body. If energy is in your chest, take a breath in and breath out *through that place in your chest.* Feel the energy dissipate as you breathe out. Notice what you are feeling and where in your body you feel it.

Thoughts and feelings can shift from one minute to the next. You may find yourself returning to the feeling check many times over the next week. Your level of distress may change as well. Add the SUDS scale to your emergency toolkit. Avoid making any decisions if you are a 5 or above, as that is a point during which we are no longer able to act (talk about our feelings) but rather we react (yelling, hysteria, rage). Use your **BREATH BREAK** and **SUDS SCALE** tool to reduce your distress to a 3 or 4 so that the logic, or thinking, brain is accessible when making decisions.

IT'S A FAMILY PROBLEM

"It is the therapist's responsibility to put the concerns of the entire family system into the equation of disclosure. How old are the children? What can the partner say to the kids to explain that she is in a state of distress? How do you help the children make sense of the pain they observe their parent experiencing?"

~ Maggie, *tenacious betrayed partner*

You may be tempted to tell your children for a number of reasons; because you are hurt, because of the unfairness of the situation; because you have always been the rule enforcer while the betrayer has been the "good guy," because you seem unstable, and many more legitimate reasons. **Remember, it is not in their best interest to know about their parent's untoward behavior as it is distressing information to children.** Generally, disclosure is not made to children if they know nothing about the sexual addiction, are not at risk for discovering it, and are under 18 years old. Most children do not want to know about their parents' sex life, let alone sexually-compulsive behavior. Parents must uphold boundaries for children and preserve their innocence. With regard to the stress in the home, children are generally resilient. They can manage uncertainty when they can make sense of the world around them. It is important to maintain as much structure at home as is possible now. Predictability provides safety for kids. Children need consistency in their daily routine, including school, homework, and activities while the emotional climate in the home is less stable. Children sense the world around them, including emotions. Typically, kids can get through difficult situations when they have a general understanding of what they see, hear and feel.

Immediate decisions that affect the children, such as agreeing that it is best for your betrayer to move into the spare bedroom, sofa or outside the home, are best handled with both parents sitting down with the children to explain the situation. What and how you discuss it depends upon their age. I do not recommend you bring sex addiction or sexually-compulsive behavior into the conversation.

Before talking with the children, you and your betrayer must agree on when changes in their routine will begin, how long they will last, if changes will affect family time, and why the change is happening now. You need to decide together what you will tell the kids. For the first six months, I suggest that changes are made on a month-to-month basis with an option to renew. It's best to be direct and specific and plan a follow-up discussion. For example, if dad will be sleeping on the sofa, let the kids know rather than "pretending" by having dad wake up early and sneak into bed before the kids wake up. It is okay for kids to know that parents struggle. It is okay for kids to know that "mommy hurt daddy" or "daddy broke mommy's trust." It is okay for kids to know that the hurt is so strong that daddy is sleeping in the spare room or that mommy is staying with Grandma and Grandpa for a month to get better. It's okay for kids to know that mommy and daddy are talking to someone about their problems and that daddy is going to his men's group to get better. Lying "for the sake of the kids" doesn't actually help the kids. *Remember that their world needs to make sense to them.* And, besides, lying was part of the problem. As with anything, check with your pediatrician if you are concerned about the wellness of your children. *Rely upon your instincts and the guidance of professionals, not solely suggestions in this book—or any other resource, including friends and family—when it comes to deciding what's best for your children.* Neither this book, nor any other should replace your own best parenting instincts and/or consultation with professionals in your area.

SPECIAL CIRCUMSTANCES

I strongly recommend avoiding the terms sex addiction, cheating, strip clubs, pornography, prostitution, affair, or any other specific descriptions unless it is unavoidable as is the case with arrests and illegal behavior. If the children must be given information for their safety, be sure to consult with a therapist that works with children or with a CSAT. Additionally, if your child lives with depression, anxiety, bullying, or any other serious illness, I recommend seeking the guidance of a qualified and licensed mental health professional.

GUIDE FOR TALKING WITH CHILDREN

Consider the guide to be a blueprint that will help you prepare for a difficult conversation. It is important to work together on this guide. You will respond to each question twice. The first response is the real, raw truth between you and your betrayer. The second response will be for the children, filtered and age-appropriate.

Describe the problem in the family

1. _____

2. _____

What is the biggest issue/problem now?

1. _____

2. _____

Describe how both of you feel about the problem

1. _____

2. _____

Who was affected by the problem?

1. _____

2. _____

Does anyone else know about the problem?

1. _____

2. _____

Is it in the kid's best interest to know who knows about the problem? Why? Why not?

1. _____

2. _____

Will there be any changes at home?

1. _____

2. _____

How long will the changes be in effect?

1. _____

2. _____

Who do you want to know about the problem? Is it okay for the kids to tell anyone? Who?

1. _____

2. _____

What are you doing to help the family heal?

1. _____

2. _____

What should everyone expect?

1. _____

2. _____

What should the kids do about the problem?

1. _____

2. _____

SELF-CARE IN THE MIDST OF A CRISIS

It is essential that you attend to your own self-care, especially if you have children at home. I am reminded of an analogy that illustrates this point beautifully. When a flight is preparing for take-off, flight attendants instruct passengers that, "In the event of a loss of cabin pressure, oxygen masks will drop from above. *If you have a child, place your oxygen mask on **before** putting on your child's mask.*" The reason for this is clear. If you attempt to put your child's mask on before your own, you will pass out from lack of oxygen and then *both you and your child are in danger.* Put your own mask on first so that you can help your children through this crisis. Although it may seem impossible, the following are the recommendations for surviving now.

- Read accurate information

  - Online—Read **credible** sources. See appendix for a list of resources for information. Avoid blogs and websites by partners, addicts, therapists who are not licensed specialists in treating people struggling with sex addiction or partner betrayal. Although tempting, some sites created by others may be more harmful than helpful. Misinformation, anger, hopelessness, and details of acting-out situations exacerbate what you are already thinking and feeling—causing even more pain. Two credible online resources are www.partnerhope.com, and www.sexandrelationshiphealing.com. See the APPENDIX for further resources.

- Exposure to information verses information seeking

  ○ Searching for more evidence of acting out is normal and helps, initially. It usually increases the intensity of thoughts and feelings that are already overwhelming to you. Information confirms your suspicions and helps you feel as safe as possible *in an unsafe situation*. Information can help to reduce fear. You can cope with what you know—it is what you don't know that scares you. If it is important for your well–being, plan time (no more than an hour, if possible) each day to probe for more information. Times and places of acting out are important for you to know. However, probing for specific acts and pictures of affair partners can cause further trauma for you.

 EXERCISE: Focus Inward

It is impossible to escape what is happening all around you. It is easy to escape what is happening inside of you. For your physical and mental health, it is essential to stay connected to your inner world. Use the writing prompts daily, if possible.

The three sentence starters along with sample responses are:

1. List something that you have gratitude for today.

   I am grateful that I am healthy today.

My response: _____

2. Describe a current challenge you are experiencing.

It's very hard to be around my betrayer's family because they don't know my secret.

My response: _____

3. List one affirming statement about you (not what you do).

I have compassion for myself.

My response: _____

I FALL APART PRIVATELY...

"For the first month after my husband admitted that he had been having an affair with one of his graduate students I could barely walk. I would be fine and then suddenly begin hysterically sobbing. My legs felt rubbery and heavy. I spent hours curled up in a ball on the floor of my closet. Being in a small, dark place helped me to calm down"

~ Serena, *betrayed partner*

Many partners report that scheduling time each day to "fall apart" was a primary coping strategy. They stated that the more their world seemed foreign to them, frightening and unsteady, the better they felt when they could control their inner "world" of thoughts and feelings. Many partners agreed that a quiet and dark space was calming.

Daily Schedule: Continue your normal routine. Tasks and activities serve to deflect and refocus attention which allows you to remain grounded—even in the eye of the storm. Your daily schedule will provide structure which will help you to feel safe.

Alcohol: Avoid excessive drinking. Having a glass of wine at the end of the day can be relaxing. Using alcohol to "get to sleep" or to reduce emotional pain actually worsens the pain and causes disturbed sleep and often leads to increased agitation and crying spells. Partners who overused alcohol say that their biggest regret is that, late into the night, they sent mean, raging texts and voice messages to their betrayer.

Humor: *Reader's Digest* has a column, "Laughter is the Best Medicine." Watch comedians on YouTube, favorite comedy programs, podcasts. Research indicates that laughter can change thinking patterns. It often reduces hopelessness, depression, and anxiety.

Exercise/Yoga: Research indicates that regular exercise helps reduce anxiety. Yoga classes can be found online, on demand through cable carriers, and through local yoga studios. Yoga can help regulate the central nervous system.

Meditation: Insight Timer, a cell phone application, has many guided meditations and various healing lectures available. Research on mindfulness meditation indicates it is helpful in reducing stress and anxiety.

Talk to Someone: As mentioned earlier, if you have a trusted friend or family member that you can count on to be a good listener without judgement and will hold your confidence, now is the time to reach out. Having someone that you can call that will listen is invaluable. Tell your friend that you need a listening ear only and be clear that you do not want or need advice. A good friend will understand. Many partners cannot tell anyone in their circle. If you are concerned that your secret will leak out, don't tell. You can always share your story but you can't retract what you have shared. Protect yourself. Use the resources provided in these pages to find a licensed therapist that specializes in betrayal trauma. Tell as few people as possible for now. Be sure that whomever you tell is trustworthy and will not share your story. Many partners have found journaling more helpful than talking to a friend.

Patience: Prepare yourself for the long game. A long-term healing strategy will yield long-term results. This will be an emotional period which may last several months. There is no fast track to healing betrayal trauma. World-renowned post-traumatic stress expert Peter Levine states that post-traumatic stress symptoms can last up to 18 months (although intensity decreases) with treatment. *Do all of the work now*. The root-level healing comes by walking straight through the emotional "fire" and facing your situation head on. It is normal to look for immediate solutions, or "band-aids." Immediate solutions help initially. The cost of immediate help to stop the pain isn't a problem until the pain returns, and by then, it is exponentially bigger. Betrayal trauma is a wound that is not easily repaired. Pain that has not been felt lurks beneath the surface.

Prayer: If you are the type of person who handles the most challenging problems, you probably believe you can fix this one on your own. If you have a religious practice, a relationship with a higher power or God, rely on it now. Reach out to your Rabbi, Pastor, Priest, Minister, Imam, Elder, Bishop, spiritual advisor, clergy or any other source that can bring even a little bit of peace. A belief in a source that you think of as a higher power can sustain you. Desperate circumstances require desperate measures.

PAUSE...BREATHE

> Breath Break: Body Scan
>
> ~
>
> Closing your eyes, focus on your breath. Breathe in through your nose for four counts and out through your mouth for eight counts. Beginning at the top of your head, slowly move down through your body noticing your forehead, ears, face, neck, shoulders, arms and continue on to your toes. If you notice energy (i.e. anxiety), breathe into it and breathe out through that place in your body. Feel the release of energy as you exhale.

A PARTNER'S WORDS OF WISDOM...

"For about six months after D-day I didn't know where to turn for help. My betrayer's therapist suggested a therapist for me who worked only with partners. What a godsend she was! She was actually a CSAT! My therapist facilitated our disclosure. When we were ready for marriage counseling, my betrayer's therapist suggested we work with him. I was so happy with my betrayer's progress that I didn't give it a second thought. I didn't even tell my therapist! What a mistake that was. From the start I felt like a third wheel. The therapist supported my spouse for his hard work getting sober and lauded him for his communication skills. Not so with me...I was criticized and corrected when I talked about how devastated I was *to learn that my spouse had several affairs and used pornography continually and excessively throughout the thirty-two years of our marriage. During one particularly heated session, the therapist turned to me and said "you are so critical and judgmental—no wonder he had affairs!" He told me that everyone knows that all men watch porn and that my husband probably used porn to get away from me!" I was shocked. When I told my therapist the story, she pointed out that I was dealing with post-traumatic stress caused by the therapist."*

~ Partner

GET THE RIGHT PROFESSIONAL HELP NOW!

The National Institute of Mental Health reports that the average delay between the onset of symptoms and receiving treatment is eleven years. People with mental illness, including depression, anxiety, PTSD, have a 40% risk of developing cardiovascular disease, diabetes, cancer, substance abuse, chronic disease, cardiometabolic disease, homelessness, and unemployment, which is twice as high as those seeking help. According to research conducted by the World Health Organization, approximately 15% of those seeking help got the right help. The International Institute for Trauma Addiction Therapists' website, www.iitap.com, includes a find a therapist function for those struggling with sex addiction and betrayal trauma. The Association of Partners of Sex Addicts Trauma Specialists website apsats.org includes a find a specialist function for betrayed partners. Faithful and True and www.newlife.com offer Christian counseling services. These organizations train and certify licensed therapists worldwide to treat betrayal trauma and sex addiction. When selecting a therapist, refer to these organizations for qualified mental health practitioners in your area.

I HAD NO IDEA!

"Three years ago, my marriage took a major detour. A detour that, unbeknownst to me, it had been on for twelve years. I discovered, through viewing information on my husband's two cell phones, he was in the grips of an addiction to online pornography. I was in shock. I was traumatized. And my soul was crushed that day. I truly was paralyzed with fear and grief. I felt like my life as I knew it had been one big lie. And, I didn't know what I didn't know. At that time, I didn't know what sex addiction was. I had no idea how to reach out for help; this felt so shameful and carried such a social stigma that I felt as though I couldn't share with anyone. What I also didn't understand is that I could actually heal from this egregious betrayal and become a stronger and complete version of myself."

~ Martha, *wise partner*

It is soul crushing to discover that your husband has kept such a complex secret life for years, maybe for your entire marriage! In the space of a moment—literally—your world, as you knew it has disappeared. Your husband's phone beeped and you picked it up expecting to read a text from your teenage daughter. What you saw at that moment you cannot unsee. Images flash through your mind constantly and, at times, seemingly out of nowhere. It's as if a thermonuclear bomb exploded in your hand. It can be paralyzing. Doing something as routine as watching a movie can cause a trauma flare as you suddenly feel your heart racing, your chest tightening, your head buzzing, fear gripping you because a scene in the movie in some way is similar to what you experienced. You are triggered and in the midst of a trauma response.

Pornography addiction is a quiet soul crusher. It is really undetectable. It can masquerade as "work." While your betrayer appears to be a diligent employee, bringing work home on evenings and weekends and working late into the night, he is likely bringing work home because he "acted out" during work hours, is acting out when everyone is asleep, or both. Although agitation and isolation make sense because "I have a deadline," these negative emotions are manipulative strategies that people struggling with sex addiction use to protect their secret behavior.

FROM A PARTNER: A PRAYER THAT SAVED ME...

"As I go through this hard time, be with me as I put one foot in front of the other. Help me care for myself. Show me simple things to be grateful for that remind me of Your goodness. Remind me it's okay not to have everything figured out right away. May I feel the feelings in the moment—no matter how sudden or painful—so they do not get stuck in my body, and may I recognize that grief is a natural reaction."

~ Rabbi R.

I REMEMBER THINKING "THIS COULDN'T BE HAPPENING"

"Imagine if one day, out of the blue, you received a phone call that changed your life. Imagine if you were on the phone and a man told you that you weren't Judy's father, that in fact HE was her father. Imagine that another man came inside me and got me pregnant. That you watched my belly grow with another man's baby. That I lied to your face, and lied by omission. That you watched a stranger's baby being born, and raised her. All of those late nights. All of the memories. Imagine learning that the daughter you love isn't actually related to you, and that your future with her is in jeopardy. How would that feel? Unlike you, my situation is not hypothetical. It is not imaginary. My situation is all too real. On April 23rd, you and I went to the pediatrician together for Judy's one year well visit. Dr. Silverman *came back into our room specifically to tell me I was a really good mom and that Judy was doing great. On April 28th, I took our daughter and a carload of stuff and I moved out of our apartment and left Chicago. I wish what happened in between was a dream, but instead it is the terrible nightmare that has been my reality since April 26th where all of my worst fears about trust and relationships have come true. I received a life-changing phone call on April 26th, the day after you were arrested for soliciting a prostitute in the third degree. I just got home from Judy's blood draw when I got a call from our best friends. They told me you were missing. Ice ran through my veins and my stomach dropped to the floor. Beth asked me if I had anyone to come stay with me. "I have no one here in Chicago," I told her. That was the truth. I had a rushing urgency to get off the phone so I could call the police. I imagined you mugged, kidnapped, in a coma in the hospital, and maybe even dead in the Chicago river like on Law and Order. Then all of a sudden you texted me, "Thanks for getting the movie tickets!" I texted you back, "Where are you? You need to call me." You told me you had a "run in with the police" and that you were getting a massage, and you "didn't say no" to a happy ending. I remember thinking that this couldn't be happening."*

~ Marnie, *truth-seeking partner to her husband*

HOW WILL I SURVIVE OVERWHELMING EMOTIONS?

Emotions are complex. They are experienced with all of our senses and are the result of how we understand, or interpret, anything at any given moment. For example, when we see a painting, our mind first makes sense of what we are looking at and then we have thoughts about it: "That's a beautiful painting." What we feel and where in our body we feel it emerges—all as a result of the meaning we make of what we see. If our mind interprets the painting as beautiful, we may feel happy, joyful, passionate, moved and we also feel the positive sensation throughout our body. We may be moved into action as a result of what we see and how we feel about what we see. In his book *Focusing*, Eugene Gendlin describes the felt sense as a physical experience of one's emotions. It is the bodily awareness of the situation, person or event. The felt sense encompasses everything we feel in the *body based on the meaning we make of what we see or hear.*

Rather than banishing feelings to some dark place in the recesses of your heart, using your emergency toolkit will enable you to manage the intensity of the feelings. Changing your interpretation (or thoughts) also changes your feelings. *Thoughts inform feelings and feelings inform behavior*—It is all connected! You can't control what is happening around you; but, with practice, you will feel more in control of what happens inside of you.

Your thoughts have the power to change how you feel. If you think of something sad, you'll likely start to feel sad. The opposite is also true: When you think of something positive and calming, you feel relaxed. Imagery techniques harness this power to reduce anxiety. For example, think of a place that you find comforting. It could be a secluded beach, your bedroom, a quiet mountaintop, or even a loud concert. For five to ten minutes, use all your senses to imagine this setting in great detail. Don't just think fleetingly about this place—imagine it. What do you see around you? What do you notice in the distance? Look all around to take in all your surroundings. Look for small details you would usually miss. What sounds can you hear? Are they soft or loud? Listen closely to everything around you. Keep listening to see if you notice any distant sounds. Are you eating or drinking something enjoyable? What is the flavor like? How does it taste? Savor all the tastes of the food or drink. What can you feel? What is the temperature like? Think of how the air feels on your skin and how your clothes feel on your body. Soak in all these sensations. What scents are present? Are they strong or faint? What does the air smell like? Take some time to appreciate the aromas.

If you feel intense anxiety, fear, or depression that does not subside using the exercises and tools, you may decide to make an appointment with your physician to request medication to help you get through the intensity of the pain. You may be opposed to medication for mental health issues for a number of reasons: the 'stigma' of mental illness, the unfairness ("Why do I need medication for your problem?"), fear of becoming a 'zombie', long-term side effects, among many others. You have survived a significant injury—a life-threatening injury. You are reading this book and seeking treatment and, in many ways, undergoing surgery to heal. Would you undergo a surgical procedure and refuse anesthesia and pain medication? If you had a headache would you take one aspirin, or half a dose? Ask yourself why you would place less importance on this catastrophic injury.

I have a problem seeking medication because _____

I could take medication if _____

Hummingbird Breath

~

Sitting comfortably, close your eyes. Focus on listening to your breath. Feel the air entering through your nose, filling up your lungs and blowing out of your mouth. Inhale slowly through your nose. Place your fingers gently on your ears to close off external sounds. Breathe out through your mouth while humming. With each out breath, hold the hummmm as long as you can. Repeat. Try a different sound such as "*Om*" or "*ohhhhhhhhhhh.*" Repeat the Hummingbird breath until your body is calm and relaxed.

I COULDN'T LOOK AT PICTURES OF US BEING HAPPY...

"I asked you if this was the first time. You said no, it's happened "a couple of times." I remember saying, "Dammit Brett, I know our sex life isn't great but you could have talked to me." You said, "I know." Somewhere in the course of that conversation you told me, "It's only hand jobs." That pissed me off to no end. I had JUST gotten a call that you were missing, I thought you were dead, and then you're trying to downplay the fact that you were cheating on me, HAD BEEN ARRESTED, and that it wasn't a big deal. More gaslighting. More emotional abuse (By the way, it wasn't JUST hand jobs.) I told you to talk to your co-worker friend since "your company thinks you are dead." I numbly put our beautiful daughter down for a nap, tried not to cry and went into action mode. I turned over all of the pictures of us in our apartment. I couldn't look at our wedding pictures or pictures of us being happy. They were all a lie, a sham. I started to cry as I gathered things in piles to pack. I started to wish you had been found dead in the river, instead of this new reality. It would be easier to deal with. I was full of rage and feelings of betrayal. I can remember almost all of the events of the next few days. Later, on D-Day, I took Alissa to the doctor to check her ear. The social worker held Alissa while I tried not to throw up in the bathroom. I told them in tears what was happening. Alissa was upset that I was crying and I tried to smile and tell her in a happy voice, 'Mommy's ok!'"

~ M., truth-seeking partner

Public exposure is any partner's worst nightmare. Brett didn't expect to be arrested when he left the house that morning or when he was caught in a massage parlor sting. His pornography habit was no longer reducing his stress—he needed something more exciting, riskier, to numb out. The majority of people with sexually compulsive behavior do not break the law. For some, the behavior escalates to paying for sex and similar behaviors discussed in more depth in chapter four "Formal Disclosure." M's reaction to Brett's arrest are symptoms of post-traumatic stress. It is important to make sense of what you are experiencing right now and to identify your symptoms so that you can use the healing trauma toolkit strategies.

Common post-traumatic stress symptoms that betrayed partners experience include:

- Feeling as though you are on "high alert" or easily startled.

- The worst part of the distressing event replays in your mind over and over again—without warning and uninvited.

- Having disturbing dreams, feeling like you are reliving the feelings of the distressing event seemingly out of nowhere.

- Feeling anxious and worried about things unrelated to the distressing event.

- Avoiding friends and family.

- Feeling numb or disconnected.

- To be upset by anything that is a reminder of the worst moment including movies, TV, books, music, while driving, or any other experience that has some type of familiarity that you may be unaware of.

- Feeling outside of your body or detached.

- Feeling foggy and having difficulty remembering everything that happened during the most distressing event or not remembering everything in order.

- Crying uncontrollably.

- Unexplained hair loss.

- Feeling suspicious of everyone.

- Losing interest in activities.

- Feeling irritable and on edge.

- Suddenly being unable to fall asleep.

- Not being able to "shake it off."

- Feeling disconnected from yourself and those around you.

- Feeling hopeless.

- Feeling guilty.

- Blaming yourself.

- Feeling shame about the behavior as though you committed it or were somehow to blame.

- Being in a state of confusion.

- Forgetfulness.

The symptoms of trauma, or post-traumatic stress, can last up to eighteen months although the acute state can persist for up to nine months. It may be hard to imagine that you will recover from this calamity; but if you commit to the work in this book, you will recover and, in the process, discover a warrior inside of you.

EXERCISE: Identifying and Managing Symptoms

As mentioned previously, knowledge provides the empowerment necessary to see the possibility that you have a choice and are able to navigate through this process rather than feeling like you are a feather floating in the wind. Knowing that you have little control of your external world, this exercise will help you to use coping strategies to manage, or control, your inner world.

Use the list of post-traumatic stress symptoms to complete the exercise below:

1. Put a check to the left of the symptoms you are currently experiencing.

2. Using the SUDS scale, rate the intensity, or pain, you experience.

3. Put the symptom in the circle that corresponds with the rating.

DISTRESS CIRCLE TENSION CIRCLE WORRY CIRCLE

(8–10)   (5–7)   (1–6)

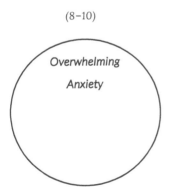
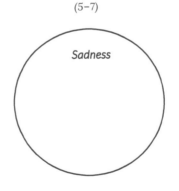
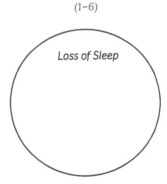

Draw your own circles. Keep a copy of your circles and stress reducers that help in your trauma healing toolkit.

A PORTION OF CAREN'S POEM...

"Through my discovery of not knowing you

I realize I have honestly not known myself

My compass was skewed and my foundation weak

I have cracked under this new weight

But I will not crumble

I need to restore my wholeness

Recovery now needs a two-lane pathway

Seeking our truths, we find our way

Out of this darkness."

~ Caren

Movement Break

~

Stand up and stomp your feet. You can stomp in place or while walking. Exaggerate your movements. Feel the movement throughout your body. Get the energy out. Stomp for at least ten minutes.

By now, you are beginning to make sense of a tiny fraction of your crisis. Maybe. Don't worry if you are still overwhelmed with emotion; remember this is a long game. Although it is natural to be consumed with the matter at hand, it is also important that you navigate your everyday life. In the words of the Chinese philosopher Lao Tzu, *"The journey of a thousand miles begins with a single step."*

It is also essential to imagine a time when you will see the light at the end of the tunnel; a time in the near future when you will feel balanced, centered, solid inside. Remember that our thoughts inform our beliefs, our feelings, and our behavior. Like the adage "You are what you eat," *you are what you think.*

 EXERCISE: My Future Reality

This exercise is one in which you will use your mind's eye to create an image of yourself in the near future. This image, or scene, will be installed deep into your consciousness—such that your thinking mind will experience the scene as real, like a memory. Although it hasn't actually happened yet, *your thinking mind will hold the scene as if it did happen.*

Because your consciousness will have the scene installed as a memory, it will feel familiar to you and, therefore, will be easy and comfortable to do again. The success of hypnosis for smoking cessation is based on the idea that we are more likely to do something difficult *if we have done it in the past* and made it through.

For this exercise you will need a pen, paper and a comfortable, quiet place. Read the visualization below, imagine the scene and then write about it.

1. Think about a situation in the near future, perhaps six months from now. Imagine that you are going about your day when you are faced with a new discovery of your unfaithful partner's secret compulsive sexual behavior. You notice that you are having a strong emotional reaction. You feel the reaction in your body.

You notice the sensation of the reaction. Is it localized in one place or does it move throughout your body? You begin to feel the feelings. Perhaps you feel anger, sadness, disappointment, fear. You notice your thoughts. You are trying to understand what you see. You are curious and perhaps confused. You realize that you are unclear and don't want to jump to conclusions and that you need more information. You take a moment to ask yourself if this is an emergency. As you think about your day, you realize that you have other and more important plans ahead and that this discovery will have to wait—and that it's okay to wait until a time that you can give this discovery your time and attention. You take a few deep breaths and agree that you can easily put the issue on hold until the evening. And with that, the feelings dissipate and you move on. Knowing that the discovery will be addressed in the evening, you notice a deep sense of peace as you realize that you are in control of your inner world of feelings and thoughts.

2. Write the scene as a story that happened to you. Write it in the present tense—as if it is happening now. Write the story with a beginning, middle, and end. Read the finished story so that it is familiar to you. Be sure that your story reflects you as empowered, strong, centered, calm, compassionate, curious. Write the story of how you will be when this is no longer the story of your life.

3. Now, move on to imagining and installing the story as a memory. Close your eyes and gently notice your breath. Notice the effortless flow of your breath and continue to do so for two minutes. When you notice a sense of inner calm, place your hands, palms down, on your thighs.

With your eyes closed, begin gently tapping the palm of your hand to your thigh one at a time, right, left, right, left. As you alternate tapping your hand to your thigh, begin bringing your story to mind.

Tell the story to yourself as if you are reading a scene from a book, just telling the story without judging or criticizing. Tell the story along with what you are feeling and where in your body you are feeling it.

Envision the story coming to life. Add what you believe to be true in the moment about you—are you wise, strong, steady, confident, resilient, and independent?

Allow at least ten minutes to thoroughly tell the story to yourself. You can use words or create a scene in your mind's eye. Take a few minutes, a few mindful breaths, and relax.

Over the next week, bring your future reality scene to mind. It will help reduce your post-traumatic stress symptoms.

FRONTLINE STRATEGY TO REDUCE EMOTIONAL FLOODING

Feelings are normal, natural, and healthy. Expect to feel overwhelmed with emotions for the next few months. At times intense feelings seem to come out of nowhere, take over and then disappear. More often, intense feelings hijack you. When feelings become so overwhelming that you feel out of control, you are being flooded with intense and strong emotions that are triggering your fight, flight, or freeze response. The fight or flight response triggers the release of stress hormones, including cortisol and adrenaline which cause physical symptoms including racing heart, tingling in your head and body, shallow breathing, dizzy, fearful, trouble thinking clearly, and unable to calm yourself down. When we are flooded, our emotions take over. The quickest way to stop the fight/flight/freeze response is to calm down—easier said than done. Exercise #3 focuses on calming the largest muscle group which is the area from the chest to the pelvic floor. Relaxing the "cheeks" (your rump, tush, rear end) really works!

Relax the Cheeks

~

Take a moment. Close your eyes. Focus on one thought...

r e l a x   t h e   c h e e k s

HOW DO I INTERACT WITH MY BETRAYER? WHAT IS NORMAL?

You are likely confused about what is best for you. A part of you may want your betrayer to support you while another part of you may want to kick him out and never see him again. The "emotional rollercoaster" will have you kicking him out in the morning and then asking him to come home an hour later, only to kick him out in the afternoon. For now, you are living in a "new" normal.

IT'S TOO EARLY TO EXPECT EMPATHY

Manage your expectations of your betrayer. You will likely feel uncomfortable with your betrayer for the first month, at least. You will feel activated. (Activation is the body's felt-sense of emotional arousal or the body's felt experience of your nervous system in action.) You may feel self-conscious, ashamed, angry, and terrified. While it is understandable to expect your betrayer to be compassionate, supportive, and comforting, it requires many skills, including the ability to feel their own pain as well as the pain of the other, which your betrayer has not developed yet. Your partner has avoided feeling intense emotions by acting out for a very long time, probably most of his life. He is learning to feel all over again. He is the most willing and the least able to offer empathy right now.

A PARTNER'S POEM

Boiled Alive

Bit by bit

Slowly, measured lies...near perfect fit

Missing hours

Explained, reframed...redirected

With flowers

Sip by sip

~ C.B.

WHY DO I NEED HELP? IT IS MY SA'S PROBLEM.

"When I first discovered my husband's addiction and his life in the shadows, I figured it was he who needed therapy, not me. Once he had connected with a therapist, it was suggested that I needed to see a counselor as well. I made an appointment with a therapist several towns away from where I lived so that I wouldn't run into anyone that would know me. The Last thing on earth I wanted anyone to know is that I needed Help! I slinked into the therapists' waiting room the day of my first appointment loaded with shame, embarrassment and fear. I have worked with this therapist for 3 years and know that this has been the key to my healing."

~ Cindy, betrayed partner

At some point, your betrayer chose to cope with stress, pressure, and emotional issues using sexually-compulsive behaviors with impunity; so it is, indeed, their problem. The profound harm caused to you and your family, though, has become your problem.

The devastation is to your life, to your emotional well-being and to your heart. Your SA'S hard work alone will not heal your pain. Partners who do not seek help continue to feel unsafe, agitated, and angry. They are easily startled, have difficulty concentrating and sleeping, and feel extremely anxious. These are all post-traumatic stress symptoms. Without help, these symptoms become a state of being; they become who you are.

The way we think has everything to do with our mental health and, ultimately, the restoration of inner peace. Any strategies, whether deep breathing, avoiding triggers, and seeking therapy when it becomes difficult to go about your usual activities of living, should be thought of as essential self-care in this life-threatening crisis. Vietnam veterans, for example, are our nation's most tragic example of the cost to those who lived through severe trauma and the long-term impact of not receiving help. Dr. Michele Spoont, a clinical and research psychologist at the Minneapolis VA Health Care System, reports that approximately 30% of veterans with untreated PTSD are more likely to have failed marriages, persistent anxiety and depression and have more medical problems. Dr. Spoont states that consequences of living with untreated PTSD get worse and worse over time. Job loss, relationship problems, explosive anger and rage, irritable bowel syndrome, digestive illnesses, heart problems, and even cancer are related to chronic stress and distress. Worse, the VA estimates that over 56% of people with untreated PTSD will become dependent on drug and/or alcohol. In the absence of help, people turn to whatever relieves pain—if only for a short time.

PEOPLE WHO LIVE THROUGH PROFOUND TRAUMA NEED PROFESSIONAL HELP TO RETURN TO HEALTH.

REMEMBER TO BREATHE.

Balloon Breaths

~

Sit comfortably, close your eyes and turn inward. Gently turn your attention to your breath. Breathing in through the nose and out through the mouth, notice the breath as it draws in and as it releases. Imagine that you are blowing up a balloon. Bring your hands up and spread your fingers around the imaginary balloon. Continue breathing as the imaginary balloon gets bigger and bigger. Imagine that you are putting a knot in the balloon. Raise your arms in the air and release the balloon!

In this chapter, you learned that the devastating crisis in your relationship has resulted in intense feelings and reactions, that you have been traumatized, and that you are suffering with post-traumatic stress symptoms. You know much of what you need to feel as safe as possible. Ahead, the confounding question "why?" (or "What were you thinking?" "How could you...?") will be explored.

CHAPTER 2

HOW COULD YOU?
(THE WHY QUESTION)

"WHAT were you thinking? Was I the only one longing to share my life with you? What makes you think you can take a stripper and her child to Disneyland, tell me, and then expect me to stand for it?

"How could you use my faith and religion against me by saying, "Aren't you supposed to forgive?" "Judge not that you yourself be judged" and, most offensive, "I think you were put on this earth to save me." Why did you even marry me? Why did you stay married to me? What does love mean to you? You obviously have no heart. How could you look me in the eyes and see how much pain I was in and how unloved I felt and continue giving our money to your girlfriend? Why did you promise me that you wouldn't ever cheat on me like my father had done? How can you say, "It's not about *you?" You told me that you never considered my feelings—Why? You admitted that you lied to your family about me, portraying me as a horrible spouse so that you would feel justified to continue your affair. Why did you need to go that far?"*

~ Daphine, *heartbroken partner*

These are the questions that every betrayed partner asks. Betrayed partners believe they cannot heal without knowing why their beloved cheated on them. They become furious when their betraying partner doesn't answer the questions, "Why did you tell me that you loved me?" "Why did you cheat?" "Why didn't you think of me when you were having sex with your affair partner?"

The painful truth is that, for a person struggling with sex addiction, there is no good reason, and for the partner, no right answer. Like the iceberg that sank the Titanic, the danger is deep below the surface for chronic betrayers.

Certified Sex Addiction Therapists' (C.S.A.T.) struggle with the same questions. Why would someone who appears to be functioning well, act against their morals and values? Are these folks sex addicted, or is sex addiction an excuse for bad behavior? The road ahead may seem daunting at this moment. The possibility that you can ever feel whole again and that your spouse will become a person that lives with integrity may seem impossible now. In my 25 years working with chronic infidelity, I can confidently state that I have witnessed remarkable transformations. I have seen miracles with couples that did not have even a thread of hope but who created a deeper and more loving relationship than I would have ever expected.

I HAD NO IDEA WHAT WAS HAPPENING RIGHT UNDER MY NOSE

"The biggest obstacle for me now is that I don't know how I can trust a person who has lied to me for 32 years—a life built on lies, deception, and betrayal. My greatest

challenge is trusting you. You don't even trust yourself to choose me. How can I trust what you say and what you do when you can justify everything you do and make excuses to make your behavior acceptable for you? I can understand how you were affected by your mentally ill parents as a child, but how you live today is your choice. I do love you, and I want to trust you again. I had no idea what was happening right under my nose. How will I ever know if you relapse?"

~ Linda, *betrayed partner*

Betrayed Partners often ask the following questions:

- What boundaries do I need now?

- Why should I stay?

- Will you relapse? What are the statistics on relapse?

- What are warning signs I should be looking for that progress isn't happening or that my unfaithful partner is acting out again?

- If you tricked me before, how do I know you aren't fooling me now?

- How can you say you love me but do what you did?

- What are the warning signs I should be looking for that you are acting out again?

- What do I need to know about your rituals to be able to recognize red flags?

- If you can't explain why you acted out, how can you possibly prevent it from happening again?

- How do you plan to assure me that this will never happen again?

Acting out with compulsive sexual behavior or sexual addiction is nearly impossible to detect. There is little evidence, if any. There is no weight gain, no weight loss, no empty whiskey bottles in the trash, no missing money. And although there is no possible way to know for sure if a person struggling with sex addiction slips or relapses, you will gain the knowledge and insight needed to trust your intuition in these pages. It is often not until the discovery of sex addiction that the betrayed partner realizes that the lies and deception dismantled their intuition long ago. Your intuitive sense is intact, and it is your inner wisdom that will protect you. Without access to your intuition, you were in survival mode. Keep in mind that if it were easily detectable, you probably wouldn't be reading this book.

TAKE A MOMENT & PAUSE.

IF IT WERE EASILY DETECTABLE,
YOU PROBABLY WOULDN'T BE READING THIS BOOK.

Re-read that sentence aloud. Say it again. Take a breath and allow yourself to take in that statement. You may disagree right now, and that is okay.

WHO AM I TO YOU?

"How are you able to lie and look me in the eyes? I must have the courage to face the fact that you were incapable of loving me unselfishly and as an equal. Was I ever an equal to

you? Were you ever attracted to me? Over time I've wondered if you ever found me appealing. Why did you have children with me? Why did you cause us financial ruin?"

~ Joseph, *betrayed partner*

Yes, the profound nature of betrayal trauma requires that you live in the painful reality that you have been betrayed by the person you've trusted the most. Painful. Often excruciating. The path to healing is to feel the pain. You will be facing harrowing truths, and your emotional and physical health requires that you face the pain. **You can't heal what you don't feel.** One truth is that your betraying partner was incapable of loving you unselfishly and as an equal. This work is not for the faint of heart.

Unfaithful partners don't understand what it means to have an intimate relationship with another person. They are very good at "acting the part," learning how to act outside like they're okay, while on the inside feeling empty, lost, unlovable, and numb. In many ways, your partner seems foreign to you, a stranger, and at the same time is your beloved. Your healing requires that you learn about the long-standing reasons that led to such extreme behavior that is likely not aligned with your betraying partner's values.

In the wake of this shocking discovery, "reasons" sound like well-crafted excuses for reprehensible behavior; that it was all a big joke at your expense—a trick. This misbelief destabilizes many partners, as they can't make sense of their reality if they believe they have been tricked and made a fool of for the betraying partner's pleasure.

REASONS ARE NEVER EXCUSES FOR BAD BEHAVIOR.
THERE ARE NO REASONS THAT WOULD EXCUSE BETRAYING THE SACRED BONDS
OF MARRIAGE AND COMMITMENT.

A person rarely remains in a long-term relationship to emotionally torment their partner. Those are usually situations involving domestic violence or intimate partner abuse and are often associated with severe mental illness such as antisocial personality disorder. Only about 2% to 4% of men and about 0.5% to 1% of women have this diagnosis.[3] Very few people in recovery from sex addiction have a diagnosis of Antisocial Personality Disorder.

 EXERCISE: Wisdom Journal

Close your eyes, turn inward and gently notice your breath. Find the place that you consider to be the core of yourself and breathe into that place. Begin to sense your wisdom source, who resides in or near this space. Connect in any way that feels comfortable for you. We all have a core of self and a wisdom source. Intense emotions consume all of our energy and push our wise advisor far below the surface of our awareness, but it is still there. Think of a wise advisor as a Dumbledore, Yoda, Gandalf, Atticus Finch. Take out your journal and reflect upon the questions Linda and Joseph asked their betrayers. *What are your questions?*

CAN I EVER FEEL SAFE WITH YOU AGAIN?

"What was your perception of the story of our lives together? What is the story you told yourself? What was it we had together? Why did I think I wasn't enough for you? Why did you lead me to believe that everything was my fault? Why did I believe your 'depression,' avoidance, and dismissal of me was my fault? Why did you allow me to

[3]http://jneurosci.org/content/36/49/12448

do things, that I am now ashamed that I did, just to make you love me? How can I ever know if you are ever acting out when you lied so effortlessly? How can you say you love me but do what you did? How can I ever believe you again? Why should I ever feel safe with you again?"

~ Nara, *betrayed partner*

Your betraying partner cannot change the past. It will take time to accept the fact that he can still love you and do what he did. I know this is difficult to get right now, but your partner's behavior will begin to make sense through the work you are undertaking. There is no excusing the choices your betraying partner made again and again. Betrayed partners who start the journey of healing described in these pages come to understand that the roots of sexual addiction begin with self-soothing in the first years of life as a means to survive an unsafe home. It will become more evident that his acting out is more about controlling an out-of-control inner world than about sex with another person. Yes, he may have texted someone and stated that he loves them, but addicts will do and say whatever it takes to hold on to the source that appears to reduce their inner turmoil. In a relationship with a person struggling with sex addiction, partners often carry the pain of years of rejection and withdrawal. In contrast, the betraying partner secretly carries the shame of feeling unloved as a child and of behavior they still use to mitigate that shame, which only causes more shame. When someone holds a lifetime of shame, it feels like a noose around their neck, and they will easily lie to cover up their behavior to circumvent being discovered.

There may be reasons for the person struggling with sexual addiction's offensive behavior, but there are *no* excuses.

"The present moment is the doorway to true calm. It is the only place you can love or awaken—the eternal present. You cannot know the future. But here and now, you can create a life of dignity and compassion, a day at a time."

~ Jack Kornfield, Ph.D.

EXERCISE: In the Present Moment

Focusing on the present moment, respond to the questions in your gratitude journal.

In the present moment:

I appreciate _____

To my left I see _____

To my right I see _____

I am frustrated by _____

I am grateful that _____

In my body, I feel _____

and I feel it in my _____

At *this very moment*, notice that there is no danger, no threat, no challenge, no decisions to be made. At *this very moment, there is no past and no future.* Practice staying in the present moment.

I THOUGHT I KNEW YOU

"This is not the person I dated for seven years and have been married to for 35 years. Are you a multiple personality? If you so skillfully hid this from me for 42 years, what else are you hiding? Do you have another family? Are we going to get a knock at the door from a child you abandoned? Are you capable of murder? I have no idea who the person who has laid next to me in bed really is."

~ Tali, *betrayal warrior*

Most partners are in such a profound state of shock that they fear that anything is possible. Even murder or child abuse suddenly seems feasible. You don't know what you don't know yet, so anything seems possible. For this reason, I urge you to seek guidance from a licensed mental health professional who specializes in treating sex addiction, as discussed in the first chapter.

So, the question becomes, "How can I ever believe you or trust you again?" Research indicates it takes about 18 months on average for a betrayed partner to be open to rebuilding relational trust after emotional or physical infidelity *if you choose to remain in your relationship*. Couples that are most likely to rebuild a healthy, strong, and intimate relationship enter the recovery process together. Marital healing after betrayal trauma is dependent upon both parties receiving the correct type of help from a professional sex addiction therapist (C.S.A.T.) who has experience working with the complexity of chronic infidelity.

When only one partner enters recovery, and the other refuses, the chances for relationship healing are slim. The betraying partner who refuses to begin therapy usually has no intention of taking responsibility for the harm they caused. Therefore, the likelihood that the marriage will succeed is low. Conversely, the betrayed partner who refuses to get help because, "This is your problem, not mine" is not taking responsibility for the impact of the harm to their mental health caused by the infidelity.

THE WEB OF DECEIT: *"CAN I EVER TRUST MY HUSBAND AGAIN?"*

"At the beginning of my journey, I wondered if a sex addict could be a loving partner. I wondered if something triggered this behavior that could possibly be cured and how I would know if my betraying partner was being honest with me. I wondered how my partner could truly love me and act out. I wondered if I would ever fully trust my partner again.

"How could I not have known? How did I miss the signs of this secret life that disregarded my feelings and disrespected everything about our marriage and family? I was overcome with rage, and I wanted to file for divorce.

"How did he get away with it for so long? How could I not have known? How could this really not be about me (doubting my attractiveness, performance, etc.) How could someone's other life be so dark and far away from the person I thought I knew? Why did you lie about things that didn't matter, like how much you spent on the Nikes?"

~ Gloria, *betrayed partner*

Soothing the Child Breath

~

In a standing position, close your eyes and focus on your breath. Feeling the air flow in through your nose, all the way down and filling up your lungs and then out through your mouth. Imagine that you have a small child in your arms and that you are soothing the child by gently swaying back and forth. As you exhale through your mouth make a quiet and steady "shhhhhh" sound. Gently swaying and exhaling "shhhhh" until you feel calm.

People who have used compulsive behaviors to manage day-to-day life develop a complex web of strategies to maintain their secret behavior. Chapter 3 discusses the roots of addiction in depth. For the purpose of the current discussion, it is helpful to understand that the need to reduce emotional pain typically begins at a very young age. Children lie because telling the truth is scarier. By adulthood, the habit of lying, deflecting, and dishonesty have become second nature. The survival strategy that enabled them to survive their childhood now causes a black hole of utter aloneness. The person struggling with sex addiction eventually exiles themselves from family, friends, and even themselves. Trapped living a double life, unable to extricate themselves from the endless cycle of seeking relief from the emotional pain (that now includes guilt and shame), the person struggling with addiction gives up the hope of a different way of life. **At its core, sex addiction is an intimacy disorder;** it is rooted in the belief that primary relationships are dangerous. Chronic betrayers fear intimacy. Sexual addiction is not about sex or love. It provides a reprieve from the excruciatingly pained feeling of intense emotions—even if it is through a computer screen in the middle of the night.

An intimacy disorder is defined as the inability to tolerate intimacy demands in a primary relationship. People with compulsive sexual behavior (CSB) don't act out to feel powerful or because they don't love their partner, but rather because these feelings leave them utterly out of control, overwhelmed, and chaotic on the inside. For these folks, fantasy and pornography are safe *because* there are no demands for intimacy, and yet, they long for closeness.

It's impossible to make sense of how your betraying partner got away with engaging in such a corrupt manner for so long, without you knowing anything about it or suspecting anything. It's also hard to accept that the person who you thought you knew so well was leading a double life.

Al Cooper described pornography on the internet as the *Triple–A Engine*: it is accessible 24/7; it is anonymous; it is affordable.[4] He called the internet the crack cocaine of sex addiction. The problem extends far beyond sex addiction. The *Triple–A Engine* has created a public health crisis. For instance:

- Research indicates that the first exposure for most males is nine years old.[5]

- 35% of all internet downloads are pornography-related.

- 25% of search engine requests are related to sex.[6]

- 70% of men and 30% of women view porn online.[7]

- In 2017 people spent nearly 4.6 billion hours on Pornhub, which breaks down to 23 *billion* visitors who watched a total of 91.9 billion videos.

- 64 billion people watch porn every day.

- 35% of all internet downloads are related to pornography.

- 40% of people identified as having "sex addiction" lose their spouses.

- 58 % suffer considerable financial losses.

- About 33% lose their jobs.

- 68% of divorce cases involve an online affair—whether or not there has been physical contact. 56% involve one party having an "obsessive interest" in pornographic websites.

[4]Journal of Sex Addiction and Compulsivity, 2004; [5]http://pubmed.ncbi.nih.gov/26175389; [6]www.covenanteyes.com/pornstats; [7]www.fightthenewdrug.org

EXERCISE: How Could I Not Know?

This question is a source of suffering. It is not a question; it is an angry challenge to the betrayer akin to "HOW COULD YOU?" It becomes a bat that betrayed partners use to beat themselves up. For them, it becomes "What's wrong with me?" Take a moment to answer that question now. Be sure to consider the big picture of your life, including children, career, and family. Many partners with families have their hands full managing day-to-day life. Continue adding to the list in your journal.

LIST ALL OF THE POSSIBLE "CLUES" THAT YOU NOW REALIZE WERE SIGNS OF SEXUAL BETRAYAL.	LIST WHAT YOU ASSUMED TO BE TRUE AT THE TIME ABOUT THE "CLUE."

Dr. Lori Gottlieb, in her weekly column in New York Magazine (May 11, 2017), *Welcome to What Your Therapist Really Thinks*, wrote a piece entitled, *"Is My Husband Having an Affair?"*

In her response to a letter from a reader, she mentions that any time somebody comes into her office to discuss infidelity, she wonders what other infidelities might be going on. Not necessarily other affairs—but the more subtle ways of straying from our partners can also threaten a marriage.

Patrick Carnes, Ph.D. in *Contrary to Love*, states his research indicates that 97% of people struggling with sexual addiction were emotionally abused as children. They were raised in unhealthy or dysfunctional homes with parents who did not or could not give them the care essential to their healthy growth and development. Poverty, mental illness, alcoholism, drug addiction, violence, or crime are among the many reasons individuals turn to sexually compulsive behavior as adults. As a result, people struggling with sex addiction have negative core beliefs about themselves. They feel alone and afraid and believe themselves to be unworthy of love; they believe that no one can truly love them because they are unlovable. Therefore, they learn from a very young age that intimacy is dangerous in real life and that they can only trust themselves to meet their needs, including their sexual needs.

In an article entitled *"Can Serial Cheaters Change?"* at www.PsychCentral.com, Dr. Linda Hatch discussed two reasons people cheat, both due to deep insecurities. Some who cheat feel intimidated by their spouse in the same way they felt threatened in their childhood homes. A *real–life connection is terrifying to someone who was not shown love as a child.* They seek affair partners, pornography, or pay for sex to avoid "real life" connection. Dr. Carnes' second book, *Don't Call It Love*, is aptly titled; acting out is not about love or sex but instead, *acting out numbs the overwhelming agony of being loved by a real–life partner.*

The "why" question matters. Is it pleasure-seeking or an escape from emotional pain? It depends. Researchers have found a link between chronic escapist distractions and negative consequences when engaged in online activities. Men who use porn to escape their lives are far more likely to experience relationship problems than men who go online for sexual pleasure. This research validates that, for people struggling with sex addiction, porn use and online sexual activities are a maladaptive coping strategy rather than a pleasure-seeking experience.

IS MY BETRAYER A NARCISSIST?

The term "narcissistic" has become a part of the common vernacular when describing people with compulsive sexual behavior. Many have traits of Narcissistic Personality Disorder, even if they don't have a clinical diagnosis. The behavior is most unquestioningly selfish and self-centered. Approximately 0.5% of people meet the diagnostic criteria for Narcissistic Personality Disorder, a diagnosis that must be diagnosed by a mental health professional. Common traits include the shameless pursuit of gratification, continual avoiding or seeking attention, perfectionism, lack of empathy for others, arrogance, disregard for others' feelings, an inability to handle criticism, and an unhealthy sense of entitlement. Most of the people struggling with sexual addiction I have worked with feel immense guilt, shame, and remorse for the harm their behavior has caused to their loved ones. If they were not addicted to the behavior, guilt and shame would prevent them from acting out in the future. Why? *Because guilt and shame guide our moral compass.*

PAUSE... & BREATHE... & AGAIN.

PRAYERS AND INSPIRATIONS THAT BETRAYED PARTNERS' DEPENDED ON DURING THEIR WORST MOMENTS

"As I go through this hard time, be with me as I put one foot in front of the other. Help me care for myself. Show me simple things to be grateful for that remind me of Your goodness. Remind me it's okay not to have everything figured out right away. May I feel the feelings in the moment—no matter how sudden or painful—so they do not get stuck in my body, and may I recognize that grief is a natural reaction."

~ Rabbi R

GASLIGHTING: ANOTHER CUT

"Why did you lie about stuff that didn't matter, like how much you spent on the Nikes? You have never had to answer to me regarding spending, and you have your own money. I have appreciated your honesty since I discovered your pornography and chat room addiction. What confuses me the most is when you told me that you would lie about little things to 'throw me off.' You talked about how good it felt when you were successful in tricking me. You confessed that, after Joseph went to college last year, when I was tearing the house apart looking for my father's watch, and you said that I told you a few days before that I put it in my winter coat and that you were worried about my memory lately, that you were just messing with me. Why did that feel good to you? I worried for months that I would end up in a nursing home wearing a diaper like my mother. The truth is that I still worry about that. You must understand what it's like to discover that your life as you knew it was unknown to you. **It is a death by a thousand cuts**. For the life of me, I can't understand how that is related to sex addiction..."

~ Anthony, *courageous betrayed spouse*

Anthony is describing gaslighting behavior. Wikipedia defines gaslighting as a form of psychological manipulation in which a person seeks to sow seeds of doubt in a targeted individual, making them question their own memory, perception, and sanity. Using persistent denial, misdirection, contradiction, and lying, gaslighting involves attempts to destabilize the victim and delegitimize the victim's belief. People use gaslighting behavior to gain control.

Stephanie Sarkis, Ph.D., in her book *Gaslighting: Recognize Manipulative and Emotionally Abusive People—and Break Free*, gives eleven ways to recognize gaslighting behavior:

1. They tell blatant lies.

2. They deny they ever said something, even though you have proof.

3. They use what is near and dear to you as ammunition.

4. They wear you down over time.

5. Their actions do not match their words.

6. They throw in positive reinforcement to confuse you.

7. They know confusion weakens people.

8. They project, accusing you of doing what they are really doing, like cheating.

9. They try to align people against you. Isolation gives them more control.

10. They tell you or others that you are crazy.

11. They tell you everyone else is a liar.

IN EARLY RECOVERY, A BETRAYER'S GASLIGHTING SOUNDS LIKE THIS...

- Why can't you just "forgive and forget"?

- Why don't you notice how hard I'm working on my recovery?

- Why aren't we having sex yet?

- I need you to feel empathy for my childhood wounds.

- When will you stop getting upset when something triggering shows on TV? It doesn't trigger me.

- Keep the secret and don't seek comfort or support from friends and family.

- Behave "normally" in front of the kids.

- I haven't acted out in months. Why don't you trust me already?

- Do not question his whereabouts or motives.

- Do not check his cell phone or computer.

- Why don't you pay more attention to me and my needs?

- It's because of my childhood. I couldn't help it because it's an addiction.

- When is it time for me to bring up my complaints about you?

- Expecting you to admit that you have problems that contributed to the acting out.

- Just accept that it is not that bad because he didn't leave you.

- Stop having feelings.

- Stop reminding me how bad I am.

- Work *your* program (a 12–step term for attending meetings).

- Pull yourself together.

- Stop threatening divorce.

- Stop trying to control him by asking how his recovery is going.

- Stop telling him what to do.

- Stop bringing "it" up because it is "shaming" him.

- Stop "nagging" (or asking for what you need).

- Take care of him.

- Believe his reason for keeping secrets was to protect you.

- That you are equally to blame and that you should take responsibility for your contribution to "our" problems.

Chronic sexual acting out is *not* an excuse for bad behavior. It is the solution, albeit temporary, for a confluence of deep-rooted childhood traumas, *perceived* relationship stress, and current issues that all collide to create intolerable distress. From this vantage point, acting out is the solution, not the problem.

Dandelion Breath Break

~

Getting into a comfortable stance, imagine that you are in a field of dandelions. Pick a dandelion. Take a deep breath in through your nose and, as you exhale, imagine holding the dandelion close to your mouth and see the white floaties drifting away. Pick another dandelion and repeat.

EXERCISE: Check-in with yourself.

Are you noticing frustration or anger? You are trying to understand *how on Earth* your beloved could have betrayed your trust, *and* you have just read about CSB, childhood dysfunction and intimacy. Let's take a moment and identify your thoughts and feelings so that they don't fester. *It is what lurks below the surface that causes suffering.*

WHAT I AM THINKING RIGHT NOW IS:	ABOUT THAT, I FEEL:	WHERE DO I FEEL IT IN MY BODY?	WHAT I WOULD RATHER THINK RIGHT NOW IS:	WHAT I WOULD RATHER FEEL RIGHT NOW IS:
EX. *Give me a break! This is a bunch of B.S.*	*Really angry!*	*Head is throbbing, pressure in chest.*	*It does seem reasonable...*	*Curious*

A BRIEF EXPLANATION OF AN INSTANCE OF CHEATING THAT IS <u>NOT</u> SEX ADDICTION

Some men and women are emotionally healthy, and they still choose to cheat. In her book, *The State of Affairs*, Esther Perel, LMFT, lists four reasons why well-adjusted men and women, happy in their relationships, still cheat, risking their marriage, home, family, job, community standing, and much more.

1. Self-exploration

2. The seductive nature of transgression

3. The allure of lives not lived

4. Feeling new or exiled emotions

Perel goes on to explain, "*People stray for a multitude of reasons, and every time I think I have heard them all, a new variation emerges. But one theme comes up repeatedly, affairs as a form of self-discovery, a quest for a new (or lost) identity. For these seekers, infidelity is less likely to be a symptom of a problem and is described as an expansive experience that involves growth, exploration, and transformation.*" These people want to escape the ropes that bind them to the daily grind for a little while—to feel young again, unburdened, and able to explore new possibilities in life. They are not looking for another person; they are trying to find who they really are or what part of them is still missing.

While this may be the case with a single affair, it is not the case with compulsive sexual behavior.

WHAT WE DO NOT FACE, LIES IN WAIT.

YOU NEED TO KNOW WHAT I NEED TO BELIEVE IN YOU...

*"You and your therapist need to know what **I need** to overcome this enormous blow. This letter may help with that process. The one undeniable need I have is for absolute honesty; I need full disclosure. I need to know that you will continue in therapy. I need to feel respected. I need to be assured that you will protect our family. I need you to tell me about your progress and also your setbacks."*

~ Joanne, betrayed partner, to her husband

BOUNDARIES

Joanne is establishing boundaries for her healing. Well-defined boundaries are the cornerstone of healthy living. Boundaries are the invisible lines that separate one from the other in all relationships. They are guideposts, rules. Personal boundaries are like geographic borders that regulate or limit the movement of people and goods into or out of a country. Geographical borders are established to protect nations.

Similarly, personal boundaries are established to protect the individual. Boundaries are essential for self-protection and self-care. It is important to identify physical, emotional, spiritual, and sexual boundaries.

Boundaries are fluid; they shift throughout the stages of one's life. In the first chapter, immediate safety boundaries were identified. In the chapters ahead, boundaries will be established for each step of the healing process. For now, it is crucial to develop comfortable boundaries so that you and your partner can continue the healing process respectfully.

EXERCISE: Establishing boundaries

It is helpful to feel calm and settled during this exercise. Take a moment to get a cup of tea. Be sure your journal and pen are nearby. With feet on the floor and sitting upright, take a deep breath in through your nostrils and hold for four counts. Exhale through your mouth for eight counts.

The following are suggestions for boundaries in each area. Choose those that work for you or create your own. Your boundaries will likely change over time. For today, begin by identifying three boundaries in each area that you are ready to enforce.

PHYSICAL BOUNDARIES—BODY

Physical boundaries refer to your personal space, body, and privacy. How close in proximity would you feel most comfortable being with your betraying partner? A foot away? Ten feet? I use a hula-hoop as a "boundary" to help define personal space between two people in the office.

My close proximity boundaries are: _____

_____

_____

What kinds of touch are comfortable? Sitting next to one another while watching TV? Hand holding? Kissing? Unexpected touch like a shoulder rub? Her arm across your shoulder? Whispering in your ear? Is it okay for your betraying partner to touch your property?

My touch boundaries are: _____

_____

_____

It is perfectly understandable if you choose no touch for now. Many partners prefer no touch during the first three to six months after discovery.

EMOTIONAL BOUNDARIES—HEART

Emotional boundaries separate your feelings from the feelings of others. They protect your emotions and your self-esteem. Emotional boundaries remind us that we cannot take on the problems and feelings of others, allowing us to be supportive without worrying about needing to fix the problem. Conversely, we can ask for help, receive emotional support, and state that questions like "Have you tried this?" are not empathetic; they do not meet your need.

Do you feel safe and comfortable sharing with your betraying partner? Do you feel comfortable sleeping with your betraying partner?

My heart boundaries are: _____

_____

_____

EMOTIONAL BOUNDARIES—PROMISES AND COMMITMENT

It is too soon to promise or commit to remaining in your relationship even though they may make promises that feel good and spark dreams of a rich new life together. If you both do your healing work, your dreams will likely be realized. Although your betraying partner is sincere at the moment, the recovery work is arduous, and they need to think and behave differently for at least six months to earn your trust. You are beginning your healing work, and your most crucial boundary is to take care of yourself. It is good self-care to do what is most difficult, which, for now, is to focus on your healing even if it means that your future is uncertain. CSAT's recommend holding off on making big decisions for the first year of treatment. You are navigating a life-changing situation and a traumatizing situation. Unless there is a concrete threat of danger, it is best to focus on your healing now.

What I am able to commit to now is: _____

_____

_____

In this chapter, we addressed the most difficult questions facing recovering couples; Why did you risk our lives with this behavior? How could you betray me? Weren't you thinking about me when you cheated on me with other people? How could you humiliate me? Wasn't I enough for you? Did you ever really love me?

You are beginning to understand that there is no real answer to these questions, or rather, no explanation makes any sense to you. We discussed some reasons people with sexually compulsive behavior betray their integrity, values, and morals. There certainly is **no excuse** for such a profound breach of your trust.

Over the past 15 years, advances in brain science confirm what we have long believed; that sex-addiction-based betrayal is equal parts dopamine, early childhood abuse/neglect, and the choice to continue cheating despite the inevitable consequences. Adding salt on the wound, gaslighting is egregious *because it is a choice*. Ahead, an in-depth exploration of these factors will be undertaken.

CHAPTER 3

UNDERSTANDING THE INNER WORLD OF A PERSON STRUGGLING WITH SEX ADDICTION

"As the saying goes, 'If you have integrity, nothing else matters; if you don't have integrity, nothing else matters.'"

~ Ruby, struggling AND strong partner

I s this sexual addiction, or is it cheating hiding under the veil of sex addiction? I have wondered that myself. Sex addiction is a term used to describe a complex pattern of thoughts, feelings, and behaviors that don't fully meet clinical criteria. Sex addiction involves a complex pattern of life-long thoughts, beliefs, and ultimately, behaviors that are rooted in trauma. The behavior is the tip of the iceberg. Above water, the behavior is attributed to stress. The danger is the glacier that lies deep below the surface. It cuts through every area of a person's life, leaving life-changing destruction in its wake.

THE THERAPIST WAS CLUELESS!

"Once my husband connected with a therapist, it was suggested that I needed to see a counselor as well. I made an appointment with a therapist several towns away from where I lived so that I wouldn't run into anyone that would know me. The first and only visit to this therapist actually added to my pain and shame. [When the therapist said] 'What's the problem, all men look at porn,' I felt like I had just fallen further down the rabbit hole into a darker abyss."

~ Martha, *wise partner*

 EXERCISE: Therapist Trauma

In the story above, Martha was shamed and traumatized by the therapist. It's difficult for many partners to see a therapist because they tend to take on their betrayer's shame and humiliation and have difficulty talking about what has happened to them with anyone. In Martha's case, the therapist's comment carried a lot of weight and deepened her shame.

Have you had a similar experience with a mental health professional? If that has been the case, you may have been traumatized. Using the questions below, take time now to process your experience.

- Describe what the therapist said to you.

- Describe the feelings you had at the time.

- How are you feeling now as you write this story?

- Is there anything you wish could have been different?

- What would you have liked to have said then?

Write the story again; this time, write the story as if it was different, as if you said what you wanted and needed to say then.

_____

_____

_____

_____

_____

_____

_____

_____

_____

IS SEX ADDICTION A CLINICAL DIAGNOSIS?

A client comes to a therapist's office because they have symptoms that interfere in their mental health, relationships, and overall well-being. The therapist's task is to determine the diagnosis that explains their symptoms. Whereas medical conditions are diagnosed and confirmed through testing (blood work, MRIs, CAT scans, X-rays, for example), mental illness is different. It is a condition of the mind, body, *and* the brain and cannot be diagnosed through traditional medical testing. Therapists rely on the client's self-report, patterns of behavior, developmental history, significant events and traumas, collateral information from family, and primary care physicians, along with the DSM[8] to determine a diagnosis. Like medicine, diagnosing mental illness helps determine the proper course of treatment.

Sexually compulsive behaviors are not easy to diagnose because the symptoms aren't easily detected. Further, there are complex processes involving several systems of the brain at work. People struggling with sex addiction don't always realize they have a problem. They assume all people do what they do or they are so detached from themselves, they are void of feeling anything. When they get help, they have a hard time figuring out why they made such destructive choices. They commonly attribute their problem to boredom, not enough sex, or no longer being in love with or attracted to their partner. The problem is that these symptoms aren't congruent with the egregiousness of the behavior—especially when separation and divorce are possible options.

People struggling with sex addiction describe preoccupation with thoughts of acting out, uncontrollable urges to do so, anxiety, agitation, mania, impulse control, depression, trauma, and erectile dysfunction, to name a few. Obsessional components of the disorder are similar to Obsessive Compulsive Disorder (OCD). Unlike OCD, either obsession or compulsion is primarily a way to manage their inner

---

[8]Diagnostic and Statistical Manual of Mental Disorders

world. Richard Leedes, Ph.D. states that the obsession is to reverie and a yearning to return to past acting out events.[9]

A long-term pattern of behavior *throughout a person's life* is considered to fall within the realm of a clinical condition such as sex addiction. Sex addiction is a common term used to describe compulsive or out of control sexual behavior. Clinical diagnoses that are common to people struggling with sex addiction include Sexual Dysfunction, Impulse-Control Disorder and ADHD. The World Health Organization defines compulsive sexual behavior disorder as a "persistent pattern of failure to control intense, repetitive sexual impulses or urges resulting in repetitive sexual behavior."

Although the link between addiction and childhood trauma was discussed in chapter 2, it is essential to revisit it within the clinical diagnosis. Gabor Mate, M.D., in his book *In the Realm of Hungry Ghosts*, states that addiction is a symptom of trauma. CSAT's treat primary symptoms such as obsession, compulsion, anxiety, and depression *at the same time* that they treat sex addiction and childhood traumas. As you are beginning to understand, people who struggle with sex addiction live with an inner system in chaos; their insides don't match their outsides.

PAUSE. BREATHE.

[9]Leedes, R., (2001) *Journal of Sexual Addiction and Compulsivity*

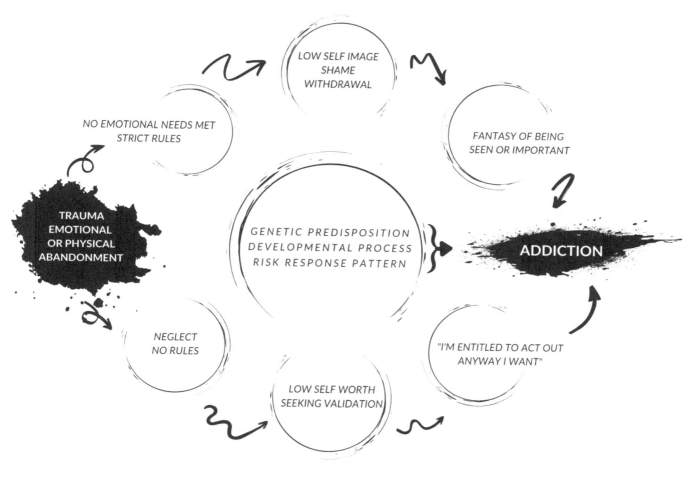

PATHS LEADING TO ADDICTION

The graphic above illustrates the relationship between attachment trauma and addiction. Emotional, sexual, or physical abuse leads to being in a state of agitated hyperarousal which often leads someone up the path of dopamine highs. Abandonment and neglect take one on the downward path of destructive entitlement.

Mindfulness Breath Break

~

Get into a comfortable position and turn your attention to your breath. Feel the air as it flows in through the nostrils and out through the mouth. You have learned that most people struggling with sex addiction also struggle with mental illness. When you feel ready, contemplate the following questions:

- How does this sit with you?

- Has your fear decreased or increased?

- Do you feel more or less worried? Are you feeling overwhelmed?

- If you are feeling more uncomfortable, journal—it helps reduce anxiety.

CAN I TRUST HIM TO BE ALONE WITH OUR KIDS?

"If he was capable of cheating and lying while looking me in the eyes, how do I know he hasn't hurt the kids?"

~ Susanna, *fully awake partner*

WHAT SEX ADDICTION IS NOT

"I couldn't help it; I'm a sex addict" has been used as a defense by criminal offenders, even murderers. To date, it has not been a successful defense because compulsive sexual behavior is not illegal. Hiring a sex worker is illegal, but *not all people who hire sex workers struggle with sex addiction.* Common assumptions to dispel are that people struggling with sex addiction are pedophiles, child molesters, "peeping Toms" (voyeurism), flashers (exhibitionism), and rapists. These are crimes. Sex crimes are intentional acts of power, control, and rage against a non-consenting victim.

 EXERCISE: Are You Worried that Your Betrayer Is an Offender?

In your journal, make a list of all of the facts—actual information that is indisputable. Next to each fact, list the source of information. When the list is complete, read through the list again. Cross out anything that you are uncertain about. Read the list one more time. After writing, rereading, editing, and rereading the list, if you are still concerned about offending behavior, talk to your therapist about your concerns.

I'M NOT SURE OF ANYTHING!

"I have so many questions. Each question leads to another. When you came back from your first appointment with the therapist and excitedly told me that you **answered** the question that has been eating me alive, I was listening. Now, I cannot wrap my head around this "answer" that it's an addiction. The truth is that I love you dearly, and I want to trust you again."

~ Val, *open-hearted partner*

THE BRAIN SCIENCE

Many mental health professionals do not believe sex addiction is a legitimate disorder. Therapists often think that the partner is the problem because they're "not enough;" not attentive enough, not available enough, not sexual enough, not thin enough, not voluptuous enough. Sex therapists (not to be confused with sex addiction therapists) believe that sexual expression is healthy—regardless of the behavior. Understanding the science that drives the addictive process is vital for your wellness, lest you take responsibility for your betrayer's acting out. Understanding the brain science that drives a process addiction is important to make sense of how something that isn't a chemical substance can be addictive.

In his book *In the Realm of Hungry Ghosts*, Gabor Mate, M.D. describes the significant role of childhood adversity and addiction, noting that early experiences play a key role in shaping a person's perceptions of the world and others. Adverse childhood experiences, or ACEs (e.g. a child being abused, violence in the family, a jailed parent, extreme stress or poverty, a rancorous divorce, an addict parent, etc.), have a significant impact on how people live their lives and their risk of addiction and mental and physical illnesses.[10]

There are two types of addictions; substance addictions and process (or behavioral) addictions. Substances, such as cocaine, cause euphoria, increased energy, and an overall sense of wellbeing. Cocaine, like all substances, enables the user to escape worries, responsibilities, and stresses. The "high" lasts between fifteen to thirty minutes, so the user must continue to consume the drug to maintain the high. As use increases, so does tolerance. The user must consume more and more to maintain the pleasurable state of euphoria. The problem is that euphoria is quickly followed by a hard-crash back into reality where the stressors still exist but are now intensified by guilt and shame for using the substance in the first place. The solution to reducing stress, guilt, and shame is short-lived and so the user must continue to use the

[10]*American Journal of Preventive Medicine*, 1998, www.cdc.gov. 2019-10-22.

substance. Because it is pleasurable, the substance increases the production of dopamine which is a naturally-occurring neurotransmitter in the brain often referred to as "a pleasure seeking chemical." Dopamine creates a reward–seeking cycle, or addiction. Dopamine causes the user to become driven to repeat pleasurable behaviors *regardless of the consequences*. Dopamine doesn't have a conscience.

Process, or behavioral addictions, refers to a maladaptive relationship with and a compulsive need to engage in a pleasurable experience such as gambling, spending, pornography, masturbation, sex, gaming, binge–watching TV shows, and high-risk experiences, to name a few.

As is the case with substances, pornography increases dopamine production. The user quickly finds themselves on the hamster wheel, seeking more exciting, more dangerous, more erotic, or more taboo material. The brain has adapted to the new normal. The brain depends on the higher level of dopamine to regulate the central nervous system. It quickly becomes the only way to reduce stressors; the person struggling with addiction ends up doing and saying things he will soon regret but cannot seem to stop on his own. Patrick Carnes, Ph.D., aptly refers to this as the *hijacked brain.*

Once the brain is hijacked, the downward spiral of craving more and more affects higher–level thinking and reasoning. Dopamine overrides almost every other system in the brain. A functional MRI (fMRI) image taken during the "high" indicates very little blood in the thinking brain so that "normal" brain functioning is essentially put on hold.

Dopamine is not bad. It ignites the fire of passion from which works of art, music, and discoveries are made. That same charge fuels addiction, disarming rational thinking, morals, values, and beliefs. When logic and reason are gone, the person struggling with addiction is in a state of no return. Tools and resources that once helped reduce stress are inaccessible. They cannot be accessed because they are replaced by justifications, rationalizations, and minimizations that make the behavior acceptable. Worse, a growing sense of entitlement emerges; the person struggling with addiction is oblivious to the dire consequences affecting himself, his family, financial stability, relationships, work, and his spiritual growth the same way a heroin addict discounts the possibility of overdose or death.

A tragic example is the death of singer-songwriter Tom Petty in 2017. He died of an accidental overdose from a combination of pain medications used to manage a fractured hip's unbearable pain. He put off hip surgery because he was finishing his final tour before retiring and felt he owed it to his bandmates and his fans to complete the tour. He was looking forward to the surgery and retirement. He didn't want to die. The pain was too great. For people struggling with sex addiction, the emotional pain becomes too great.

PAUSE. TAKE A BREATH.

Mindfulness Breath Break

~

Sitting in a comfortable position, close your eyes and focus on the flow of your breath, in through the nostrils and out through the mouth. Ask yourself, "What is my greatest strength?" Take a few minutes to answer that question.

THE RECIPE FOR SEXUAL COMPULSION

Those struggling with sexual compulsivity have felt unloved and unworthy for much of their lives, *even though they have partners who love them.* The development of intrinsic worth and value develops based on how caregivers related to children in their earliest years of life. These early experiences go on to shape lifelong attitudes, beliefs, and behaviors. These core beliefs influence relationships, friendships, and careers. The majority of caregivers are well-meaning and do the best they can, given their circumstances. If children get enough care and attention, they emerge from childhood feeling strong, confident, and worthy of love. Children who do not get their basic needs met, however, have life-long difficulties forming close attachments.

For the child, imagining a family where they feel important and loved becomes a way to nurture themselves. For the child who feels lonely and insignificant, the real world is unsafe. Without mom's attentiveness, the child believes they are unworthy of acceptance. In their make-believe world, "good" mom is always available, loving, and happy. "Good" mom becomes a comforting fantasy in which the isolated child feels safe and loved. In the "real" world, the child believes themselves to be flawed, unworthy, and unlovable. In the fantasy world, they are essential and valued.

Understandably, the child chooses to spend time with their imagined "good" mom, especially after the child suffers abuse by "real" mom. Over time, the child develops a close attachment to the surrogate "good" mom. Because the primary caregiver models the expectation for subsequent close relationships, "good" mom sets a high bar for future partners. Real people cannot live up to the ideal, fantasy woman, and the person struggling with sex addiction yearns for a close attachment to their beloved. There are two truths; (1) A longing to love and be loved, and (2) A belief that close connection is dangerous. The early attachment wound makes it impossible to sustain a close and intimate connection.

Wounded children develop behaviors that help them escape from the pain, relentless negative judgment of themselves, as well as fear, self–criticism, and perceived rejection by others. They learned from a young age that they are on their own. They miss critical developmental hurdles, including learning how to cope in stressful situations, tolerate complicated feelings, and the importance of asking for help. They believe people to be unreliable and untrustworthy. "Acting out" is a primitive way to self–soothe. In *Facing the Shadow*, Dr. Patrick Carnes describes a *behavior pattern that develops to manage inner suffering* as the sex addiction cycle.

THE SEX ADDICTION CYCLE

The eternal cycle of sexual acting out begins with feelings. Overwhelming feelings of any kind have the potential to send someone into the addiction cycle. Those who resort to using any means to tolerate intolerable feelings do so because there is a part of them that becomes utterly overwhelmed in any intense feeling state. The only solution that helps *without fail* is the habit of fantasizing or obsessing on something other than the feelings. In this way, acting out is understood to be a solution rather than a problem. It is easy to understand why someone who has no tolerance for negative feelings would act out. Getting a raise at work, landing a sweet deal, or any other achievement can be excruciating for people who believe themselves to be unworthy or unlovable. *People with sexually compulsive behavior can "act out" on a good day or a bad day.*

Preoccupation through fantasizing or obsessing is an attempt to make intolerable feelings disappear by "checking out," detaching, or floating away through a trance–like state." Once in this state, the person becomes a prisoner of their obsessive thoughts.

Obsessive thoughts increase excitement and increase the production of dopamine in the brain. The same is true for drugs and alcohol. The person struggling with cocaine addiction is on a dopamine "high" on their way to buy the drug. *They were high on dopamine before the drug entered their system!* This naturally-occurring, pleasure–seeking chemical in the brain is so powerful that it is nearly impossible to interrupt once stimulated. Think of dopamine as being like a train. Once the train leaves the station, there is no turning back. The only way off the train is to wait for the next stop.

Obsessive thoughts, or preoccupation, lead to ritualization. Rituals are a predictable pattern of behaviors developed over time to intensify obsession, increasing excitement and arousal. Most importantly, though, it provides a sense of control for someone who feels utterly out of control. Rituals are the method used to "act out." They may include preparation such as having alcohol, searching the internet, cruising, cleaning the house, or any other behavior that becomes part of the routine. The rituals ultimately serve to deflect from intense feelings of worthlessness, guilt, shame, and inadequacy.

Acting out is the final phase of the cycle. It is often the shortest phase and, for many, the least exciting. By this time, the dopamine level has depleted, and excitement is replaced by detachment and apathy. An immediate feeling of hopelessness, despair, shame, and helplessness set in.

Feeling a deep sense of failure along with the belief that "I am bad" deepens despair, sending the person back into the vicious cycle of addiction. The suffering is so profound that it often leads to thoughts of hopelessness and suicide; and so, acting out is the only way out of the pain.

I THOUGHT LOVE LETTERS ARE A DEEPER EXPRESSION OF LOVE...

"What's with the love letters while you were having an affair? Why did you cause me the deepest despair, writing me love letters? Why did you write me love letters? What is love? What did it mean for you to be loved by me? Did you value the honesty of my love?"

~ Tony, betrayed partner

To further understand, let's return briefly to the origin of the problem. The first five years of life shape the very foundation of a human being. Our caregivers, or family of origin, have everything to do with how we come to understand ourselves and make sense of our world throughout our lives. John Bowlby, M.D., published his research on the significance of the child–mother relationship in his groundbreaking book *Attachment: Attachment and Loss, Volume 1*. Dr. Bowlby concluded that the critical period for the development of secure attachment occurs within the first two years of life. The disruption of that natural bond causes lifelong difficulties forming trusting relationships. The first two years of life are critical to the child's sense of trust and safety.

Receptor sites in the infant's brain are awaiting mother's loving gaze. This all-important gaze reassures the infant that she is a separate person who is valued and loved. That mother is dependable and readily accessible. The mother's dependability teaches the baby that the world is safe and that caregivers are trustworthy. Through the "gaze," the baby develops a secure attachment to the mother/primary caregiver, *who is the most significant first relationship in the infant's life*. In these first two years, the baby needs a "good enough" mother to thrive.

Because babies cannot survive without their caregivers, a consistently unreliable mother causes anxiety and fear in her baby because their very survival is at stake!

When a baby grows up with unstable mothering, the baby can't predict when its most basic needs, including food and comfort, will arrive. This unpredictability results in the baby developing an anxious and insecure attachment to the mother. Sensing that mother cannot be depended on, the child learns to soothe itself in whatever way works. Suppose a mother cannot attend to her baby during its first two years of life for whatever reason (poverty, war, depression, e.g.). In that case, the window of opportunity closes and cannot be repaired, and the child will seek that elusive "gaze," or approval, for the rest of their lives. In her groundbreaking book *Not Just Friends*, Dr. Shirley Glass describes it as "having adoration mirrored back at you."

People who compulsively act out with others look to the love-struck eyes of an affair partner to meet that unfulfilled need. They are drawn in by the gaze. It is the experience of seeing themselves mirrored back through the other's adoring eyes that they are in love with! Although your partner loves you, when another person offers the "gaze," the betraying partner suddenly feels loveable. They feel "seen" and they see self-worth reflected at them. In this way, acting out creates a false sense of value and importance.

It does not excuse their behavior. The most prevalent reason people become addicted to sex or porn is because of what Dr. Glass describes as "the desperate search to heal the 'mother wound,'" to finally be "seen," worthy, and loveable for no reason other than being *the very one that they are*. The tragedy is that the experience of being seen in that unique way is utterly impossible to relive. The gaze attunes infant to mother; in harmony and in sync. The absence of Mother's gaze cannot be replaced because the infant has begun adapting to the abandonment because mother is unreliable. As a result, the child has difficulty navigating friendships and relationships because they don't feel safe; they feel unworthy and unlovable and terrified of abandonment. More information on attachment, the mother wound, and the affects on adult relationships can be found at www.positivepsychology.com/attachment-theory.

PAUSE AND BREATHE.

 EXERCISE: Journal Entry

In your journal, begin a list of any questions you have about sex addiction, sexual compulsion, your betrayer's childhood trauma, and any other questions that come to mind. Leave several pages blank so that you can continue adding to the list.

HOW DOES AN ADULT WITH A MOTHER WOUND UNDERSTAND LOVE?

This is an excellent question that goes to the heart of the life-long consequence of early childhood neglect and abuse. For these people, love has become intertwined with fear and danger. They yearn to be loved. They long to have an intimate relationship. Holding hands while walking on the beach and spontaneous getaways are opportunities for intimacy. For chronic betrayer's, love is demanding and smothering. Many chronic betrayers say that they lose a part of themselves in a relationship; for them, love involves danger, submission, and sacrifice. They feel overwhelmed and that they can never "get it right." Over time the acting out behavior becomes the best solution to the problem of feeling invisible and lost.

Healthy relationships are ones in which each person respects one another's values. They enjoy their hobbies, interests, and preferences. They follow their passion without fear of disapproval or control by the other. They can be honest and forthright because they trust that their partner will respect them.

They can compromise on important issues. In healthy relationships, people can ask for what they need; they expect to have their needs met. They can give and receive love and be vulnerable because they trust their partner to love them for who they are, warts and all.

The chapter ahead will be painful. If you and your betrayer have sought help from a CSAT/Partner specialist, within approximately six months your therapists will suggest a Formal Disclosure, a process where your betrayer admits to all of their sexual behavior, lies, and secrets. Although agonizing to relive the nightmare of those first days and weeks, it begins a new phase in your personal growth as well as healing the relationship.

FRONT—LINE SURVIVAL TOOL

Planning ahead so that your world is predictable dramatically reduces the possibility of another ambush. It allows you to run a scenario with all of the possible triggers so that you are in control of your mental health. Before moving on to the next chapter, set goals for yourself that are feasible. Take charge of your world and your trauma symptoms by planning, predicting possible triggers, and setting a daily schedule that will support your healing.

EXERCISE: Goal Setting

Daily and weekly goals are essential in the first three months. Create a goal for the day every day and an action goal for the week. Choose goals that are feasible considering your current circumstance.

Examples from recovering spouses:

"For the first week my goal for the day was to eat and breathe" ~ Nira

"Daily goals literally kept me sane in the beginning. Getting out of my pajamas, taking the dog for a walk and remembering to breathe were my go to goals in the beginning."

~ Shanice

"I set daily, weekly and monthly goals. They actually were my lifeline in my first year of healing. In the beginning they were as simple as brush your teeth and take a shower. My weekly goals were focused on doing something for myself which, at the time, were Netflix binges, listening to comedy podcasts and Zentangles. My monthly goals helped with deadlines." ~ Heather

"Honestly, my goals early on were about keeping my job! Return emails and calls, submitting expense reports, and getting to work on time" ~ Darryl

My goal for the day is: _____

_____

My goal for the week is: _____

_____

_____

"Everything can be taken from a man but one thing: the last of the human freedoms—to choose one's attitude in any given set of circumstances, to choose one's own way."

~Viktor Frankl, *Man's Search for Meaning*

CULTIVATING HOPE

In his book *Late Great Planet Earth*, Hal Lindsay wrote, "Man can live about forty days without food, about three days without water, about eight minutes without air...but only a second without hope." Hope is a state of mind that is built on an expectation that something better lies ahead. Dr. Frankl, a Holocaust survivor, observed that those people who perished collapsed into themselves, believing this was their fate. Those who survived, including him, believed they would be reunited with their families.

🦉 EXERCISE: Statement of Hope

Write a confident statement of hope. Print a copy to carry with you as a reminder. Write it on a Post-it and put it on your bathroom mirror.

_____

_____

_____

_____

_____

_____

_____

CHAPTER 4

FORMAL DISCLOSURE

Take a few minutes to reflect on what you have learned so far: you have tools to regulate your moods and challenge your negative thoughts; you understand some of the factors that set the stage for your betrayer's choices and decisions; and you learned how distressing childhood events shape the essential development of a human being. Most important, you learned that an essential part of your healing is to get *the right* professional help.

You have the foundation needed to weather the storm ahead. Expect this to be a difficult and painful process. Be sure your goals are reasonable and that they are for your healing only. It is time to get the truth and face the reality of your life head on. Your betraying partner will prepare and then read a document fully admitting to all of his secret behavior. If your betrayer is willing and you choose to go through this process, the pain of the first discovery will descend upon you; an avalanche of anguish, hurt, sorrow, horror, and confusion will return with an intensity that may feel worse than "D–Day."

CRITICAL MOMENT

DO NOT RUSH INTO THE DISCLOSURE PROCESS. DISCUSS DISCLOSURE WITH YOUR CSAT/PARTNER THERAPIST TO BE SURE THAT YOU HAVE THE BANDWIDTH TO COPE WITH A SECOND TIDAL WAVE OF PAIN.

YOU ARE ENTITLED TO DISCLOSURE AT ANY TIME, BUT YOU CANNOT UNDO THE DAMAGE IF YOU ARE NOT EMOTIONALLY READY.

"During [treatment], my husband shared an accountability letter in which he owned the way he lied and deceived me for most of our 32 years of marriage. It was so difficult to hear him say these words, and I cried uncontrollably as he spoke... Since then, my husband and I have completed our disclosure process, including his full admission and accountability of all of his acting out behaviors."

~ Stronger and more confident betrayed partner

Formal disclosure begins the process of relationship healing. Betrayal breaches foundational trust in a relationship. Without trust, there is no safety and no basis on which to move forward. You are entitled to know the truth about your relationship and the person with whom you have spent most of your life. Whether or not you choose to participate in a formal disclosure, this chapter will move you through the process so that you will know what to expect.

Formal disclosures are recommended even when your betrayer states that he has "told you everything." **There is always more.** People who have been chronically unfaithful rarely confess when caught. It is the mental illness; the addict part is in action right before your eyes, lying, minimizing, blaming others. They "go down with the ship," admitting only to what was discovered. It is human nature to protect oneself from *perceived* danger or attack.

Decide if and when you want disclosure. I recommend that you and your CSAT or CPTT (Certified Partner Trauma Therapist) discuss and plan ahead, knowing that this will cause an emotional setback. Planning at the outset is important. As your betrayer faces the impact of his decisions on you, guilt and shame take over. Believing he is helping you, he may confess to you a little bit at a time when you are least prepared. Although you may be desperate for the truth, it can set you back emotionally. *Learning about betrayal is traumatizing because you are caught off guard.* These unplanned events are referred to as staggered disclosures, and each one will feel like stepping on a landmine. It is best to insist that the betrayer waits until the formal disclosure to reveal new information for your *emotional health.*

HOW SOON SHOULD DISCLOSURE HAPPEN?

I recommend that formal disclosure is facilitated within the first six months of treatment, typically in the fourth to sixth month, barring complex circumstances. The betrayer needs to have built the capacity to be honest for the disclosure to be meaningful. Although partners expect disclosure immediately upon beginning therapy, it is unlikely that your betraying partner will be forthcoming until then. The idea of waiting even a minute longer for the truth is frustrating for partners. I work with many partners offended by the notion, believing that the cheater will be indulged at their expense.

To tolerate holding off, let's dispel myths about disclosure.

TEN COMMON MYTHS ABOUT DISCLOSURE ARE:

1. People struggling with sex addiction are more likely to be honest if confronted because they don't have time to come up with a lie.

    TRUTH: *People who have something to hide will employ any emergency tool to get out of perceived danger, including shutting down.*

2. Betrayers are master manipulators who easily dupe therapists into believing the partner is at fault.

    TRUTH: *While that may be the case with a non-specialist, CSAT's are trained to help betrayers to learn healthy ways to get their needs met.*

3. If the betrayed partner agrees to wait for disclosure, it gives the betrayer the impression that he is off the hook.

    TRUTH: *If the betrayer is in treatment with a CSAT and follows the treatment, he is on the hook. Treatment is focused on the infidelity and harm he caused you.*

4. Betrayers con therapists into believing that the *real* truth will cause too much harm to their partner.

    TRUTH: *CSATs know that the betrayer is worried about the harm telling the real truth will have on them. CSATs teach them to feel the pain.*

5. The therapist is trying to control the situation.

    TRUTH: *The CSAT therapists collaborate to mitigate re-traumatizing the partner. If the betraying partner is not ready to be honest, it would be D-Day all over again. They control the situation to prevent further suffering.*

6.   The partner knows everything and doesn't need a formal disclosure.

     TRUTH: *The betrayer rarely admits to the full extent of their behavior.*

7.   The betrayed partner will appear weak and pathetic if she agrees to wait.

     TRUTH: *Reflecting on this, isn't it curious that an act of self-care (waiting for the whole truth) is viewed as a weakness rather than a strength? This question is a reflection of the long-term impact of gaslighting (Chapter 2) which leaves the partner questioning her reality.*

8.   The only way to empower themselves is to have a disclosure on their terms (in the privacy of their own home).

     TRUTH: *Disclosure in and of itself is an act of empowerment. It occurs in your therapist's office, with questions that you provide, and with the betrayer's therapist—who will call him out if he minimizes or omits information.*

9.   Confronting the betrayer at length when he is vulnerable and unsuspecting, like an interrogation, is the best way to get at the truth.

     TRUTH: *Human beings as a species survived because of our "lizard brain," a term for the oldest and most primitive part of our brain that keeps us alive. When a threat of danger is perceived, the lizard brain (near the brainstem) sends a warning signal throughout the body to prepare for an attack using it's weapons; fight, flight, freeze or appease. Human beings cannot be in a state of fear and have a conversation—let alone a confrontation.*

10. The betrayer is a "pathological liar" who is incapable of telling the truth.

     TRUTH: *Chronic betrayers are expert liars. Betrayers lie more frequently than they act out. As long as the behavior is secret, they lie and omit such that they believe their lies! In recovery, betrayers work hard to be honest and transparent.*

The formal disclosure process is complicated, for sure. We have no way of predicting how it will unfold and its impact on you, which is why it is important to discuss it with your therapist. In their book *Disclosing Secrets*, Deb Corley, Ph.D. and Jennifer Schneider, M.D (2002) report that their research indicates that, over time 96% of people struggling with sexual addiction and 93% of partners come to believe that it was the right thing to do.

Expect to feel as distressed as you did on the day of discovery. The closer you feel toward your betrayer, the worse you will feel after disclosure. Prepare yourself to take a few steps back in your emotional recovery. Whether you have discovered or were told everything, it is excruciating to hear it all at once.

WHY DOES MY HUSBAND NEED A THERAPIST TO BE FORTHRIGHT WITH ME?

Your husband is breaking a life–long habit of dishonesty and deception to you and also to himself. Your unfaithful partner needs to develop trust in his therapist and break down the intricate system of denial built and fortified with each new lie. His dishonesty probably spans many years. He will go through a rigorous process of honesty and self–reflection in preparation for formal disclosure. You have been waiting a long time, and it is likely excruciating. Believing that disclosure is the key to calming overwhelming fear and anxiety, a rushed disclosure often results in further harm to you and damage to the relationship. Worse, it leads to more revelations and more suffering. Remember, your betrayer has built a sophisticated system to deny that his behavior was hurtful or wrong. He is literally in denial of the fact that he is in denial!

In my experience over 25 years of facilitating disclosures, betrayers are more likely to be honest, forthcoming, and transparent when they have worked with a CSAT for at least three months.

CSATs create the safety and trust needed to be honest. Although CSATs are highly trained and qualified specialists, it is essential to state that no therapist can or should guarantee that the betrayer is 100% honest. Their knowledge and expertise guides betrayers *who want to heal* through the muck of lies and deceit to get to their truth. The majority of people who seek help for cheating want to get better and they will do whatever is needed to help their partner heal.

YOU DESERVE TO RECEIVE A THOUGHTFUL AND PLANNED DISCLOSURE THAT IS "ONE AND DONE."

An additional major roadblock to moving forward is the belief that the cheater does not empathize or grasp the magnitude of the harm and its impact in many areas of your life. Long-standing betrayal affects you as well as the family system as a whole. Your betrayer must face the consequences of his choices so that healing can begin, and the reality is that it will take time for empathy to come naturally. *If they were capable of empathy, they wouldn't resort to acting out in sex addiction.*

WARNING: THE EXERCISES IN THIS CHAPTER AIM TO HELP PREPARE FOR A THERAPIST-LED FORMAL DISCLOSURE WITH A QUALIFIED MENTAL HEALTH PROFESSIONAL. THE AUTHORS DO NOT INTEND THAT IT BE USED FOR A SELF-LED DISCLOSURE. IT COULD DO CONSIDERABLE DAMAGE WITH INAPPROPRIATE USE.

THE THERAPIST-LED FORMAL DISCLOSURE PROCESS

Two conditions are optimal for healing: (1) That the formal disclosure occurs between three to six months of entering treatment, and (2) That it be facilitated by CSAT's, or certified partner trauma therapists. Remember, this is what they specialize in. Would you let your family doctor perform open heart surgery on you?

I've witnessed partnerships fail because, before they arrived in my office, the betrayed partner was blamed, shamed, labeled, diagnosed, and, worse, marginalized. Licensed therapists who are untrained to treat complex issues, including chronic cheating, sexual compulsion, attachment wounds, mental illness, *and* a traumatized partner in crisis and falling apart at the seams, can cause severe trauma. Therapist-induced trauma is another betrayal.

We strongly **do not recommend** *doing disclosure on your own because you believe you can't wait (you can!), or the betraying partner insists. This is a serious mental health situation; admitting and hearing the scope of the lies can send people into a depression or worse, contemplate taking their lives.*

HOW WILL I KNOW WHEN I AM READY?

When you and your betrayer feel safe and trusting of your therapists, your healing journeys begin. Practice the strategies and the acute pain will start to subside a few months after discovery. As you feel more balanced, you will know when *you* are ready for disclosure. *Disclosure is for you.* The therapists collaborate throughout the process to ensure, as best as they can, safety and honesty, so there will be no secrets, manipulation, avoidance, and any other means people use to avoid pain.

The formal disclosure itself is a four-step process that occurs over the course of two therapy sessions. Preparation for disclosure can take up to six weeks, as your betrayer's therapist holds up the mirror of reality so that your betrayer faces the full extent of their acting out behavior.

The betrayer will prepare:

- A thoughtful and thorough response to all of your questions.

- A Sexual History Timeline listing all instances of unfaithfulness, including:

  - List of *general* addictive behaviors.

  - List of *specific* addictive behaviors, including:

    - Time frames of acting out (dates and events).

    - Frequency/duration of acting out.

    - Money spent on acting out.

    - Behaviors that have involved another person/people.

- Identity of any acting out partner that you may *personally* know.

- Identity of any friends/family members who may already be aware of this problem.

- Information starting from when you first were involved with your partner. Many partners find it helpful to receive information about the full history of sexually compulsive behavior from the time it began.

- All legal issues including arrests, civil lawsuits, stalkers, extortion, sexually-transmitted diseases, pregnancies, job losses.

I strongly discourage disclosing specifics about each instance, as it will create a scene in your mind that will haunt you. Many partners insist upon knowing every detail, including descriptions of people, sexual acting out behavior with them, or pornography viewed, for example. Others insist that the betrayer show them websites, physical places, or names and phone numbers of affair partners, if any. *Viewing the actual website, physical location, or even speaking to an affair partner never* ends well. Affair partners are usually embittered. When a betrayed partner confronts them, they often go off the rails with anger, insults, shame, mocking, and devaluing because they believe themselves to be the rejected, injured party. The information will further traumatize you. **You cannot unsee the scene that will be created in your mind or unhear the horrible words you hear; they will replay over and over and over, re-traumatizing you every time.**

GUIDING PRINCIPLE OF PARTNER HEALING:

LISTEN TO YOUR INNER WISDOM TO KNOW WHAT IS IN YOUR BEST INTEREST. DISCLOSURE IS FOR YOU.

IN PREPARATION FOR THE FIRST DISCLOSURE SESSION

- Cancel your schedule for the day. You will not want to go to work or take care of anyone for the rest of the day.

- Plan in advance for a quiet day. Make arrangements for work, family, and any other responsibilities on the day of disclosure.

- Give thought to what will be most helpful for you after disclosure.

- Partners suggestions include:

    ○ Arranging dinner with a friend that knows the situation.

    ○ Meeting with your group members for dinner.

    ○ Scheduling a session with your therapist after disclosure.

    ○ Agree that the betrayer will take care of home and family responsibilities.

- o Indulge yourself with a stay in a hotel with a spa to schedule a spa treatment, sit in a hot tub, or a tub with bubbles in your room and to order room service.

- o Have music, readings, candles, oils, and anything that is soothing nearby.

- Bring a pad of paper and a pen with you to write down anything that you are thinking and feeling during the process and any questions that arise during the disclosure.

- Drive separately to the session.

- Wear comfortable clothing and bring anything with you that is a source of soothing.

THE FIRST THERAPIST–LED FULL DISCLOSURE SESSION

Your safety in the disclosure is *the essential* need in the process. For this reason, the partner's therapist facilitates formal disclosure in their office. Chairs are situated, so you and your betrayer sit across from each other, eye to eye and heart to heart. Your therapist is seated nearby to facilitate the session, and the betrayer's therapist is sitting nearby as a supportive observer.

As you begin the session, have something to drink, a pad of paper, a pen, and a box of tissues. It is best to listen without interruption. Write down any questions that arise rather than asking at the moment. It is difficult not to interrupt, but it is less stressful.

The session begins with the betrayer admitting to the full nature of his wrongs in his sexual history timeline. Wrongs refer to his cheating, harmful actions, feelings, and beliefs that justify that those actions were somehow acceptable. All unfaithful behavior, including the frequency of each behavior and the amount of money spent, will be stated.

Your betraying partner will read and respond to all of your questions. Ask any questions that have come up that require further clarification. Avoid questions that involve provocative details of cheating or that are veiled and angry attacks. It may feel good at the moment but has a short half-life and will only intensify your anger and discouragement.

You will then read your impact statement to your partner. Provide your betrayer and his therapist a copy of your impact letter. Afterward, your betrayer will need to write an emotional restitution letter to you.

The session ends at that point. It is a painful and exhausting experience, and it is also a turning point moment for both of you. Feel the feelings and face straight into the pain because you have to walk into the fire to get to that other side where you reclaim yourself. Allow yourself to *feel* it.

SECOND SESSION: POST-DISCLOSURE (1–2 weeks after formal disclosure)

In the second session, your betrayer will read his emotional restitution letter to you. The emotional restitution letter will be an opportunity to gauge your betrayer's progress in treatment; is he more transparent, forthcoming, and honest? Do his actions align with his words? Is he following the CSAT's treatment plan? Do you see vulnerability and remorse? The seeds of trust are laid in the second session.

PAUSE & TAKE A BREATH BREAK.

"D–Day: the day I discovered the truth about my husband was the worst day of my life. The shock, the disbelief, the fear, and the anger were completely overwhelming."

~ Stronger and more confident betrayed partner

 EXERCISE: Preparation for Disclosure

Make a cup of tea and reflect on the time since your D-Day. Use the workbook exercises and journal entries. Put pen to paper, and start writing whatever comes out without editing or holding back.

1. Close your eyes and be quiet with the question:

    "What do I need to know to feel safe?"

Take time and be thorough with this exercise. Disclosure is an extremely painful process. Asking questions post-disclosure prolongs the suffering unnecessarily.

The Information I need is:

a. _____

b. _____

c. _____

d. _____

e. _____

Use your journal to write more about the most crucial information that you need from your betrayer in his disclosure.

---

2.   Close your eyes and be quiet with the question:

"Going forward—beginning at the end of the session—what do I need from my betraying partner to feel safe?"

The boundaries I need to establish to feel safe are:

a. _____

b. _____

c. _____

d. _____

e. _____

Use your journal to write more about boundaries. Boundaries are a line in the sand. They are the door that protects anyone from entering without invitation because the doorknob is on the inside, your "no-fly zone." What are you unwilling to tolerate? These boundaries will change as you feel more comfortable and safe, but until then, what do you need from your betrayer that you will include in your impact letter?

My *Partners In Healing* group states that you need to know:

- The type of behavior: cheating with others, either paid or unpaid, or using the computer to access material to view or even others online.

- The progression of the actions—how bad did it get and when?

- Were there protected or unprotected sex acts?

- The type of acts engaged online or elsewhere.

- Anyone else that knows.

- Illegal behavior.

- Arrests.

- Any lies or deception that has not been previously admitted.

- What triggers the cheating?

- What strategies does the betrayer have to prevent a relapse?

- Do you want information starting from when you first were involved as a couple?

- Do you want information regarding sexual compulsion through your betraying partner's entire life?

WITHOUT EXCEPTION, PARTNERS IMPLORE YOU NOT TO ASK FOR THE "GORY" DETAILS OF SEXUAL ACTING OUT!

The following is a list of commonly asked questions and items in formal disclosure:

- List all of the cheating behaviors. Please include the number of instances, when they occurred, and the amount of money you spent on each occurrence.

- How long have you been acting out?

- When did it start?

- How did you meet people to act out with?

- Did you tell the acting out partner anything about me?

- How did you avoid being caught? When did you act out? Was I home?

- Did you act out in our home? Where? How? How many times? When? Where was I?

- Does anyone know about your secret? Do any of our friends or family know?

- Have you had sexual contact of any kind with anyone I know? Describe the situation and with whom you acted out.

- Have you ever been arrested? On what charge? When? What was the outcome?

- Have you ever tried to stop or get help?

- Have you lost a job or professional opportunity due to your acting out?

- Do you have another family or children? Where? Describe the situation, including financial, emotional, and time spent.

- Did you go on vacation or travel with your affair partner?

- Have you ever committed a crime? Describe.

- Why did you marry me?

- Why didn't you break up with me?

- Did you ever love me?

- Have you acted out or have any secrets you haven't admitted?

An essential component of relational healing for betrayed partners is being adequately heard and understood for *the full extent* of the pain wrought by their betrayer's decisions and choices. Is there anything else you want to know or say?

I have facilitated disclosures where the partner had five questions. Another had 40 questions and sub-questions, as well as partners that didn't want the information at all. Ask for what you need, within reason. Your drive to finally hear the truth can also cause self-harm, which won't hit you *until after the disclosure*. It would be best if you *cared* for yourself like never before. It is essential to your well-being because the mind and the body are connected. Fear and intense worry release cortisol and other stress hormones in the body, leading to health problems including: high blood pressure, headaches, adrenal fatigue, weight gain, weight loss, panic attacks, sleeplessness, and depression.

 EXERCISE: Self-Care

Read the self-care strategies in the appendix. List five actions that you are willing to do this week to release the built up pain and stress. Your recovery and health depend on it.

1. _____

2. _____

3. _____

4. _____

5. _____

"My impact letter detailed the numerous times I had been traumatized and damaged by his addiction, and his emotional restitution was his first step toward empathy. Guided by our wonderfully-skilled therapists, we came through the process with renewed hope for our future."

~ Accepting and hopeful betrayed partner

IMPACT LETTER

In preparation for formal disclosure, you will be encouraged to write an impact letter. The letter to your partner/spouse will describe the impact of the cheating on you and your family in a non-critical and non-shaming way.

The letter must include specific examples of actual experiences you have had. The betrayer will reflect on the reality of those situations and have a new awareness of your pain. The letter should include facts, feelings, and outcomes.

The letter will probably require revisions. The letter's impact is most potent and most effective when issues and facts are presented *without* judgment or criticism.

"We had a formal disclosure planned, which was not easy in the middle of a pandemic. I worked on my impact letter for about a month. I was so angry that I raged in my first two drafts. I tamed it down because I realized that it wasn't going to get me what I needed—the truth. The weekend before the disclosure, my betrayer insisted that we didn't need to spend so much money on therapists. He said that since we were ready, why not do it at home? We did, and it was 100 times worse than discovery. There was new information even though he insisted that I knew everything. He ended up raging at me!!!"

~ Susanne, smarter and wiser betrayed partner

EXERCISE: Impact Letter Practice

First draft: Practice impact letters help many betrayed partners reduce distress and gain perspective and clarity about what is needed in disclosure to move forward. In this exercise, you will write a draft of your impact letter. **However much you may want to read the letter to your betrayer now, DON'T. You will be letting your betrayer off the hook**. The betrayers' therapist may never know about it. Accountability and responsibility for the harm caused is diluted because the atmosphere is much more comfortable at home—especially because there will be no annoying therapists to challenge omissions.

GUIDELINES

- Please write the letter in the first person, using "I" statements and being as specific as possible.

- Please limit the letter to no more than six to ten pages.

The following is a suggested outline for the preparation of the letter. Feel free to use the guideline as it feels useful for you. Each numbered item may be the beginning of a paragraph.

1. First, write about the discovery of the behavior. Write about how your world was shattered, changed, impacted. How did you react? How did your spouse/partner react?

2. How did you handle the information initially? What was running through your mind?

3. Write about the next day, week, month. What was life like? How did you carry on with work, family, and other responsibilities?

4. Write about the emotions you felt. What did you think of yourself, your body, your worth as a spouse/mate? What did you believe to be true about you at that time?

5. How do you feel about the lying, hiding, deception, manipulation? How do these impact your trust and safety in the relationship?

6. Does the lying impact your self-esteem?

7. Discuss the impact on your sexuality, desirability. Do you feel rejected sexually?

8. Do you feel upset about the information that your spouse's recovering friends have that you do not (acting out specifics or details)?

9. Does anyone in your life know about the betrayal? Write about what impact not sharing the "secret" has had on you. Do you feel like a liar, a secret-keeper, a fraud?

10. Do you lie for your spouse/partner to keep the "secret"?

11. How have your life and your family, friends, work, children been affected?

12. Write about the broken fantasy of the life you thought you had and about your lifetime expectations of marriage.

13. Have you been used as an excuse or blamed for your spouse's behavior?

14. Write about how you question everything and have become hyper-vigilant due to the lies.

15. Write about any events in the past that you questioned at the time.

16. Write about how your spouse/partner's avoidance physically, emotionally, and spiritually has impacted you. If your betrayer has withheld affection or sexual intimacy, describe what you have believed to be true about you.

17. Describe what it was like living with your betrayer before discovery. Were you lonely? Describe holidays and other special events that were affected by the betrayal.

18. Closing—state your wants, needs, hopes, and wishes for yourself, your relationship, and your betraying partner.

Reminder: This letter is part of a therapist-led formal disclosure. The letter's intention is twofold: (1) To express the full extent of harm caused by betrayal trauma and (2) To enable your betrayer to become fully empathetic to your trauma. Avoid editing your thoughts and feelings as it potentially mitigates the letter's impact and, ultimately, your healing and the healing of the relationship.

This process may be painful and bring up unexpected feelings. It is best to write this letter with the support of your therapist, group members, recovery friends, or trusted friends.

"To me, trust and truth are the foundations of a good marriage. I'm not willing to compromise myself where they are concerned."

~ Cautious, betrayed partner

FINAL EXERCISE: A Second Look at Your Needs

1. What are you hoping to receive by hearing your partner's disclosure?

2. Is there specific information you need?

3. Is there any information you do NOT want?

4. How will you feel if your betrayer discloses more than you anticipated?

5. What is your biggest fear about formal disclosure?

6. Are you ambivalent about staying in the relationship?

7. What are your deal breakers for moving forward in the relationship?

8. Is there anything you could hear in the disclosure that would cause you to want to leave the relationship?

9. Are you dealing with thoughts of harming yourself or others?

IF YOU ARE THINKING ABOUT HARMING YOURSELF OR SOMEONE ELSE,
GET PROFESSIONAL HELP NOW.

"Within the first month after the discovery of sex addiction, it would have been helpful to know others had experienced this disease. I needed to understand this compulsion with VALID information. I needed to be reassured a lot that I did not deserve this situation. And such a concept needed to be drilled into my head! I was

not physically able to seek this out myself; I was depleted, in shock, and scared. My google searches on "sex addiction" opened up a frightening world of "deeds" I had never heard of that left me obsessively wondering and worried about what else my husband was lying about. I read with horror the pain of other betrayed partners. I ingested the vitriol in many, many partners, the intensity of which I could not fathom. I needed to know what was safe to read, watch on TV, and read online.

"I needed to know how important it was to work with a therapist that understands sex addiction and is specially trained. I needed to know that therapists that aren't trained will blame me because; all guys watch porn and that I'm making a big deal about it as a way of not having sex; It's my fault because I'm a nag; I have too much anger (that really made me angry!!) and, worse of all, told me I was making a big deal of it and I was too sensitive. I would have liked hearing that it was possible to get out of the deep marriage hole of going-through-the-motions type marriage into something better.

"When I discovered your acting out and asked you about it, I believed you when you said it must have been our son that was looking at porn at all hours of the night. I remember how shocked he was when we confronted him and how angry he became after that. I feel like such a fool.

"I remember that night. I woke up at 4:00 in the morning with a start. I'm not sure if it was a dream or a sign from above. I had a sense that something was very wrong. Out of the blue came your gut-wrenching betrayal. You abandoned us for your own selfish perversions. My everyday existence was a struggle. I questioned how you, the person believed in and trusted more than any other could do such a thing."

~ Linda, *goddess warrior*

THE HEROES' JOURNEY: THE PATH TO HEALING

Linda needed a wise guide—a mentor. She needed to know what she needed in order to face the formidable foes of betrayal, trauma and sexual compulsion. In an instant, her world as she knew it vanished, dissolved. Linda needed a roadmap. She needed to know what trials and obstacles were around the bend. Allow your workbook to be a guide and your therapist to be your mentor.

Like Linda, you were living your life as you knew it. When the infidelity was discovered, it catapulted you into a crisis. At this point, there are two paths ahead and you are facing a dilemma, a crossroads, a fork in the road, a decision. The path on the left is the well-worn path of refusal and denial which leads back to your life as you knew it; but a darker version of your life. By choosing the uncharted path on the right, you accept the call to action and with it a commitment to growth and wisdom. Joseph Campbell describes the hero's journey as a "challenge or quest that presents itself to an ordinary person in an ordinary world. With guidance, they cross the threshold and commit to the journey and overcome their fears. Their ordeal forces them to face their worst fears and, [ultimately] becomes a painful evolution to dignity, wisdom, and inner strength."

"I was invited to share my wisdom because I was where you are right now in 2012. After I discovered my husband's secret life, I ran to treatment. Actually, my husband and I ran to treatment. I found Michele and she referred my husband to her colleague. I immediately joined their Partners in Healing group and my husband joined their Foundations group. We worked hard the first year and followed every treatment recommendation. He embraced S.A., sponsor, steps, R.C.A., workbooks, and formal disclosure. I'm not going to kid you—I felt like I was back at D-Day. Our relationship became stronger and we were more connected than we had ever been. After a year and a half of working on myself like it was a full-time

job and raising six kids, as hard as it was, it felt like the right time to leave group and see Michele if anything came up.

"All I can say is that it was good until it wasn't good anymore. My husband continued in his recovery work, became a sponsor, spoke at meetings and conferences, and continued to grow. One day, five years later, I was standing at the kitchen sink and began to cry. Nothing happened to speak of. All I can say is that I slid downhill very quickly. I was depressed, had panic attacks, and felt like I had a 20-pound weighted blanket over me. I called Michele and got back into therapy.

"I learned the hard way that stopping therapy after disclosure tucked the pain into some dark place. All it took to pull the lid off the box was my husband telling me that he and his sponsor decided to start an S.A. meeting a couple of hours away in an outlying area. As he got better, I felt like I was in quicksand. It took me a couple of years of therapy and medication to climb out of that hole. My wise words to you who are walking the path—do your work now and don't stop until you get to the other side!"

~ Sarit, *wise partner in healing*

Your heroes' journey begins now. You will battle dragons, depraved monsters, and the dark side of your betrayer. Stay on this journey and you will come through to the other side.

EXERCISE: Securing the Tools for Your Heroes' Journey

- Your journal and special pen

- Your gratitude journal

- A grounding object. Your palm stone or other small objects that are comforting to the touch

- Affirmations

- A compassionate heart for yourself

- Time set aside each day for workbook

- One act of self-care daily

CHAPTER 5

HEALING YOUR TATTERED HEART

"I can be changed by what happens to me, but I refuse to be reduced by it."

~ Maya Angelou

Previous chapters focused on what happened to you, how to make sense of it, how to survive moment to moment, and preparing to face the truth of your betrayers' infidelity. You will not have all of the information or answers about your betraying partner's decisions and actions until a CSAT-facilitated full disclosure occurs. Keep in mind that information will *not* be the source of your healing.

You may believe that you can't or shouldn't stop focusing on your betrayer's acting out behaviors and that, if you do, they might relapse. It may seem impossible, but now is the time to intentionally shift your attention to your own healing.

Partners who continue to be consumed with seeking information are tortured—not by the behavior but by their unrelenting quest to uncover all of the lies. Searching for information or signs of acting out quickly becomes all-consuming. Information-seeking helped to decrease the panic and the horrible loss of power that was taken from you after discovery. Intense emotions and unreliable thinking became a force from within which fueled anger, rage, and revenge; and the powerful energy inside was like a runaway train gaining speed until it crashed. It became a bottomless pit. Linda, a betrayed partner, described it as descending into a "pit of shit." Hurt, anger, embarrassment, fear, and rage create intense pressure which is relieved, temporarily, by investigating. The problem is that now, each instance of checking creates more anxiety, questions, and pressure. Rage, fear, obsession, and shame became your new reality. Over time, the intense feeling states lead to an entrenched sense of embitterment. It becomes the lens through which everything is experienced.

The fact is that no amount of checking cell phones, emails, social media, etc., will prevent a relapse. Worse, it does not reduce your anguish or your heartache, and it does not give you your old life back. Before moving ahead, put pen to paper and write about your thoughts, feelings, fears, and beliefs about the following statement:

DO YOU WANT THIS TO BE **THE** STORY OF YOUR LIFE OR **A** STORY OF YOUR LIFE?

Will this tragedy become *the* story of your life? If the answer is yes, take time to reflect on how an embittered life will look 2 years, 5 years, 15 years from now.

EXERCISE: Write Your Story

Take time now to write what happened to you. Write everything that comes to mind.

EXERCISE: A Vision for Me. Who Will I Be?

Write a self-statement, a vision for yourself. Who will you become as a result of slaying dragons, confronting your fears and reclaiming your core self?

THERE IS MORE THAN ONE TRUTH

A guiding principle of healing is that *there is more than one truth* in any situation. For instance, one part of you might be devastated by your partner's infidelity, another fearful of a relapse, another part that is hopeful for the future, another enraged at their carelessness, and a part that holds deep love for them all at the same time. In addition, you feel deflated, self-conscious, guilty, ashamed, etc. All of these feelings and beliefs live in the same body. Understanding your own parts is essential for this expedition inward.

EXERCISE: My Truths

Identify and list the many truths living within.

_____

_____

_____

_____

_____

WHY IS IT IMPORTANT TO SEE YOURSELF AS A BUNCH OF PARTS?

Why did this happen to me? That is an excellent question. You will arrive at your answer through your heroes' journey. First, allow yourself to take that 18-inch drop from your head to your heart to feel what is happening to you. It is crucial to keep track of what is happening inside. Did you know that thoughts often inform feelings? Thoughts such as "No wonder this happened, just look at me!" lead to feelings of shame and self-loathing. Because those feelings are too much to bear, people usually withdraw and numb out.

A mugging, identity theft, a disagreement that turns into a violent exchange are good examples of traumatic events that happen to us. The discovery of sexually compulsive behavior, or the popular term sex addiction, is rarely planned by your betrayer. In my 23 years working with people struggling with sex addiction, less than 5% of my clients have admitted that they have been unfaithful; 95% admit to infidelity only after they have been caught, lied and denied as long as they could, and finally broke down, admitting everything.

"Ring the bells that still can ring, forget your perfect offering, there's a crack in everything, that's how the light gets in."

~ Leonard Cohen

WHAT WAS REAL?

There is much that was and is real. It is natural and understandable to question everything. Although, in the first year after discovery, it is challenging to believe that anything was real. You certainly can't depend on what a person struggling with sex addiction says. It will be at least a year before you can trust them, which comes only after a sustained, consistent, and verifiable period of honesty. As difficult as it is, this is a question best asked after about a year of recovery. What your betrayer offers at this time will likely be infuriating. In my experience, partners can discern, in time, what was real. Suppose your partner admits to his problem and seeks appropriate help, and follows the treatment recommendations. You will likely experience a person who is more anxious, depressed, agitated, robotic, needy, overly-attentive—a very different person than he was before discovery. At this time, you will be able to have meaningful and satisfying conversations about what was real.

Since the discovery of your partner's deception, It may feel like everything is tainted. "I don't know" responses are painful and infuriating. For many partners, this fortifies the belief that "I was never important" and worsens your 'new' insecurity, and lowers your self-esteem. If there were any benefit in asking this question, I would recommend it wholeheartedly.

Partners live with a unique paradox. A part of you is angry, sad, hurt, enraged, outraged, confused, mistrusting, and suspicious—and horrified! That part of you does not believe that you can ever feel safe or trust your betrayer—and with good cause. Another part of you needs what only you believe your betrayer can provide: comfort, understanding, validation that you are still loved, and validation that you are desired. The dilemma is common. The paradox here is that there is a need to seek comfort from the very one who has caused the pain. In no other "life-threatening" event is one compelled to seek comfort from the source of the trauma. The problem here is that your betrayer cannot give you the compassion and empathy that you so desperately need. Many partners say, "He needs to heal me; it's his job to heal me; after all, he caused it—he should have empathy for me." In marital sessions, the partner will look at me with exacerbation, demanding that I "back them up" and chastise the SA for behaving selfishly.

Although it is difficult to understand and believe, people struggling with sex addiction are *incapable* of feeling and expressing deep compassion. If your betrayer was able, he would not have engaged in harmful and possibly life-threatening behavior. People who love themselves do not engage in such behavior. People who love themselves treat themselves well and with respect. Remember, engaging in dangerous and secret sexual behavior is abusing themselves. It is a desperate measure to reduce overwhelming pain. In no way is this a condoning of such conduct; it is, however, a fact. The fact that a person engages in behavior contrary to their moral system of values is the best measure of a lack of compassion for themselves. If one believes themselves to be bad, worthless, and unworthy, they are in a state of self-hatred. Compassion for others is a state of love and respect. If one does not love and respect themselves, how is it possible to do so for another? Their habit was built over the years and years and years and years of compulsive sexual behavior. With each event of acting out, two things are reinforced: (1) That the action consistently works to relieve pain, and (2) That the betrayer believes themselves to be horrible, disgusting, dirty, a fraud, shameful and unlovable. It is impossible to have compassion for someone else if there is no compassion for one's self.

HOW DO I MANAGE MY MEMORIES?

Reflect on what was meaningful for you. If your memories include your children and loved ones, they are genuine. Memories are built upon hundreds of precious moments. Together, these memories make up the story of your life. These memories are the story of your family. Each moment is complicated, unique, and invaluable and ought not to be treated carelessly or defined if it is real by the one who betrayed your trust.

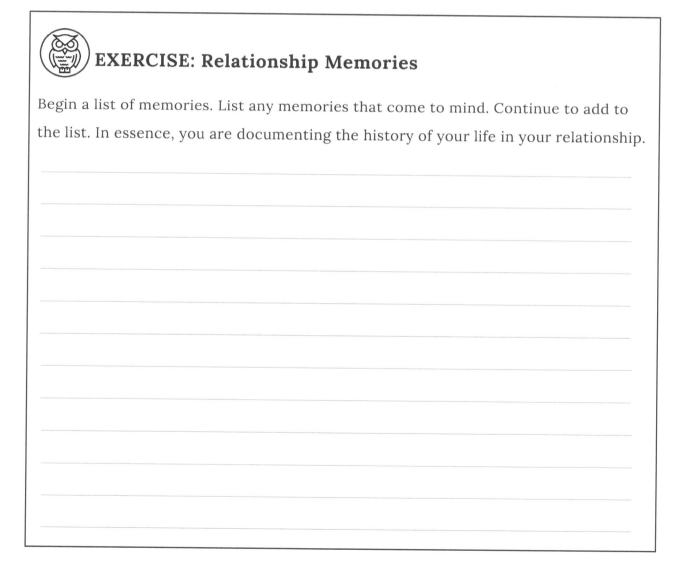

EXERCISE: Relationship Memories

Begin a list of memories. List any memories that come to mind. Continue to add to the list. In essence, you are documenting the history of your life in your relationship.

GENTLE EXPECTATIONS OF YOURSELF

Your primary focus is maintaining emotional stability during the shock and chaos of discovery. Reduce your commitments for now. Let go of "shoulds." Cross off items from your "to-do" list. Use gentle distractions to manage the pain. Overuse of distraction (binge-watching on Netflix, over-exercising, beginning a big project) may lead to repression or avoidance of the pain. The first three months after discovery are fluid. Partners continue seeking information after discovery through research and asking their betrayer questions. More information is likely to be disclosed. Utilize the self-care tools in the appendix often.

THE DILEMMA OF PEOPLE STRUGGLING WITH SEX ADDICTION

Many people struggling with sex addictions respect and understand that their choices and behaviors are the cause of your distress. To aid in your healing, they work to remain sober, return to mental health and defer to you. They work hard to respond to you with sympathy. They work hard to imagine what you must be going through (although not very well in the first year). The 12-step program coaches them to "seek to understand before needing to be understood" (Prayer of Saint Francis of Assisi). Through the recovery process, people struggling with sex addiction realize that they fear conflict and avoid confrontation at all costs. They have difficulty clearly stating their frustrations as well as their needs. They come to realize that they rarely, if ever, addressed challenges in their relationships. As they continue on their recovery path with therapy, readings, and 12-step meetings, they work hard in therapy to understand their feelings. They learn what they need and how to express it to their partners. The good news is that relationships become stronger and more intimate, connected and attentive. Many realize that one of the contributing factors to their sickness was that they couldn't "use their voice" when upset. Instead, they avoided difficult situations by "acting out." The less they addressed problems, the more resentment they accrued. People struggling with sex addiction overwhelmingly report that they want to take responsibility for the harms they caused and learn how to listen attentively. Betrayers realize that they will be triggered and incorrectly believe that they have "no voice."

EXERCISE: Self Check-In

Having read the betrayer's dilemma, list what you are feeling and where in your body you are feeling it right now.

_____

_____

_____

_____

_____

EMERGENCY TOOLKIT STRATEGY

PLACE HAND ON STOMACH, BELOW THE DIAPHRAGM

INHALE AS HAND GOES OUT

EXHALE AS HAND GOES IN

HOW CAN I MAKE IT TILL BEDTIME?

"What does a broken heart feel like? Kick to the gut. And another one. And another one... no time to catch my breath before another one comes. A baseball bat across the side of my head at full force. Short of breath, headache, sweating, nausea, tightness in my throat and stomach. Heavy eyes from not sleeping and constantly crying. Closing my eyes and feeling the horror of betrayal by someone I loved above all else. Living every waking moment in the nightmare that feels like someone else's life, but it's really mine. Trying to make the pain stop but no idea how to do it. Wondering if tomorrow will be a little bit easier to face and struggle through. And then it isn't. How do I stay standing every day? How can I make it till bedtime tomorrow without collapsing? How is it possible that any shattered heart is still beating? Why is this happening to me? I just want to die."

~ Brave betrayed partner

One of the most painful truths is that there is no "fixing" the situation. You can't "fast-forward" through the pain. The healing comes by walking straight into the fire until you reach the other side. Walk head-on into the storm. Remember, mental health is facing your reality at all costs.

 EXERCISE: Journaling Revisited

Dr. James Pennebaker's research indicate that journaling daily elevates the immune system, calms the autonomic nervous system, reduces heart rate, slow breathing, and reduces fear. The purpose is to understand your inner world. Journaling allows emotions that may have been pushed underground to emerge. Journaling enables our thinking to become more transparent. Journaling allows the mind to integrate thoughts and feelings along with traumatic experiences.

Journal for ten minutes everyday. Allow your thoughts and feelings to flow onto paper without editing.

The Chinese character for crisis is a combination of two words: danger and opportunity. Betrayed partners state that one of the most challenging issues is facing or "leaning into" concerns that need to be addressed. In your journal, list the conversations that didn't happen or that you did not say what needed to be said, but, for some reason, you held back.

*"I got my **own** back."*

~ Maya Angelou

Empowerment begins with reevaluating the situation with an expanded perspective. We start with the understanding. There are at least three truths in every story: your side, the other person's side, and the story as told by an observer. Taking back our power requires that we look at all sides of the issue. As difficult as it is to imagine that you may have a "side," the painful truth is that we all do.

Gentle reminder: the next exercise in no way implies that you have responsibility for your beloved to have betrayed you.

EXERCISE: Taking Back My Power

You will need your journal for this next exercise. In your journal, write the story of what happened to you. Write about the lie that impacted you the most. Write about the way the lie has changed how you think, believe, and feel about yourself. What is the story you tell yourself about why your beloved betrayed you? When finished, reflect on your journaling by answering the questions in the space provided.

What is the lie in the story that I tell myself? What is the truth in the story that I tell myself?

_____

_____

_____

What is the most significant hurt I have suffered?

_____

_____

_____

How have I allowed that hurt to control me?

_____

_____

_____

What am I not allowing myself to face?

_____

_____

_____

What do I fear most would happen if I face it?

_____

_____

_____

How will my betrayer feel toward me if I face it?

_____

_____

_____

If there is a part of me that believes I had a role in my hurt, write about it.

_____

_____

_____

What questions do I continue to ask myself?

_____

_____

_____

What is blocking me from letting the questions go?

_____

_____

_____

My greatest fear about my story is...

_____

_____

_____

What did the betrayal take from me?

_____

_____

_____

Although a part of me wishes the betrayal never happened, I now understand...

_____

_____

_____

What am I willing to forgive myself for?

_____

_____

_____

What truth about my betrayer have I had to face?

_____

_____

_____

What I cannot make peace with is....

_____

_____

_____

What I am willing to do with what I cannot make peace with is...

_____

_____

_____

Reread your story. Reflect on your responses and rewrite your story. Allow the new information to influence your story.

What hurt me the most upon the discovery of betrayal?

1. _____

2. _____

3. _____

NAME THE HURT

What was most devastating about the hurt?

_____

_____

_____

It hurts me the most because?

_____

_____

_____

What I have the most difficulty with today is...

_____

_____

_____

Who can I talk to that will understand and not judge me or give advice?

_____

_____

_____

I have been devastated by the discovery, but it will not...

What the discovery of betrayal took from me was...

What my betraying partner took from me was...

What scares me the most right now is...

I am holding in...

I am most afraid to say...

_____

_____

_____

What I need to be safe right now is...

_____

_____

_____

What has helped me to feel safe in the past when I've been in crisis is...

_____

_____

_____

What I need right now from my betraying partner to feel safe is...

_____

_____

_____

I keep wondering why...

_____

_____

_____

How have I allowed the hurt, anger, and fear to control me?

I can't give it up because...

 EXERCISE: Self-Reflection

The head and the heart aren't always in sync. You have read explanations about why your life partner cheated, that chronic cheating doesn't happen because of something you did or didn't do, and you have read the brain science about compulsive behavior. Your heart probably doesn't agree with all that you have read so far. It is okay for you to disagree! It is important that your beliefs are a part of the process of making sense of this calamity; after all, it is *your* life. Your emotional healing begins with respecting your truth along with the information in these pages.

The intention of the exercise is to get all of your thoughts on paper, regardless of whether they are "right" or "wrong" because they are right for you at this point.

YOUR THOUGHTS AND FEELINGS MATTER.

Why did this happen to me?

_____

_____

_____

Why this bomb?

_____

_____

_____

Why now?

_____

_____

_____

What is the message or lesson for me?

_____

_____

_____

What wasn't I seeing?

_____

_____

_____

What was I accepting or depriving myself of?

_____

_____

_____

Did I really have the life I thought I did?

_____

_____

_____

How has this changed my life?

_____

_____

_____

TOLERATING UNCERTAINTY

Many partners state that, by far, the most painful part of the discovery of their betrayer's"acting out" is the overwhelming sense of uncertainty. When we are highly anxious, we tend to overestimate the level of danger we are in and underestimate our ability to cope with what we most fear will happen. The shocking experience of discovery, accompanied by the belief that there is more to be discovered, is certainly an expectation that the worst is not over.

The level of fear combined with the experience of uncertainty increases worries and fear thoughts. The mistaken belief is that we can reduce uncertainty by worrying about it. The phenomenon of the "intolerance of uncertainty" raises anxiety to overwhelming proportions—such that you believe you cannot cope with not knowing everything. Anxiety and fear are extraordinarily high; the mind races with fear thoughts such as, "What else don't I know" and "What is he capable of?" create the belief that "I must be 100% certain" to feel safe, thus igniting obsessive information-seeking. The greater the worry, the greater the need to be in control, yet information-seeking increases fear. It does not ensure the end of adverse events, secrets, or emotional pain.

The fact is that it is highly likely that you do not know the full extent of the egregious behavior. Proclamations of honesty don't increase safety at this state of your recovery. Verifiable facts are reliable, dependable. Although information-seeking is often referred to as detective work, it is the best way to gauge safety. Attempts to control anything (your betrayer's whereabouts, for example) only increase fear and anxiety exponentially.

Surviving this period of uncertainty, confusion, suspicion, fear, and broken-heartedness requires being able to tolerate the rollercoaster of emotions and cope with this not-knowing in ways that will sustain strength, wellness, and emotional health.

Use tools and strategies often, try to stay off the emotional rollercoaster of fear and anxiety. Tara Brach's RAIN of Self-Compassion, Carol Vivyan's APPLE acronym, my Breath Break exercises and Marsha Linehan's Wise Mind exercise are front-line interventions to disrupt anxiety-driven obsession.

Practice the tools often so that they become intuitive.

THE RAIN OF SELF-COMPASSION

In her book *Radical Acceptance*, Tara Brach states, *"In order to unfold, self-compassion depends on honest, direct contact with our vulnerability. This compassion fully blossoms when we actively offer care to ourselves. Yet when we've gotten stuck in the trance of unworthiness, it often feels impossible to arouse self-compassion. To help people address feelings of insecurity and unworthiness, I like to share a meditation I call the RAIN of Self-Compassion."*

The acronym RAIN is an easy-to-remember tool for practicing mindfulness and self-compassion using the following four steps:

- **R**ecognize what is going on.

- **A**llow the experience to be there, just as it is.

- **I**nvestigate with interest and care.

- **N**urture with self-compassion.

CAROL VIVYAN'S APPLE ACRONYM: *(GETSELFHELP.CO.UK)*

- **A**cknowledge—Notice and acknowledge the uncertainty as it comes to mind.

- **P**ause—Don't react as you normally do. Don't react at all. Just pause and breathe.

- **P**ull Back—Tell yourself this is just the worry talking. This apparent need for certainty is not helpful and unnecessary.

- **L**et Go—Let go of the thought or feeling about needing certainty. Tell yourself it is only a thought or feeling. *Don't believe everything you think!* Thoughts are not statements of fact. They will pass. You don't have to respond to them. You might imagine them floating away in a bubble or cloud.

- **E**xplore—You can explore the present moment because right now, at this moment, we are ok.

Mindfulness Breath Break

~

Notice your breathing and the sensations of breathing. Notice the ground beneath you, look around you and notice what you see, what you hear, what you can touch, what you can smell right now. *Shift your focus of attention* to something else—on what you need to do, what you were doing before you noticed the worrying thought, or do *something else*—mindfully, with your full attention.

MAKING DECISIONS WITH A TRAUMATIZED BRAIN

"I think; therefore, I am."

~Rene Descartes, *French mathematician and philosopher (1596–1650)*

Our ability to think and remember the past sets us apart from any other species. Animals react to the world around them. We human beings reflect on the past and take feelings into consideration when making decisions about the present or future. Our intellect, reasoning, past experiences, memories, feelings, and our ability to imagine the future together enable us to make complex decisions, make choices and develop and achieve goals.

Our sophisticated system works well *except* when it is in a highly-charged emotional state. In this state, our thinking is unreliable because our feelings drive it. Intense emotions often override logic and reason. When we feel fierce compassion, we spend more money than we can afford on gifts and donations. When we are in an intensely angry state, we may impulsively quit a job or end a relationship. In both examples, emotion overrides logic. Decisions regarding how to think and feel are made in the brain's frontal cortex.

The frontal cortex is made up of two hemispheres. The left hemisphere, or thinking mind, is responsible for analytic thought, order, computation, detail, rational thought, and logic. The right hemisphere, or emotion mind, is visual and intuitive. It is responsible for creativity, imagination, intuition, and feelings. Thoughts inform feelings. Hope-filled thoughts lead to joy. Worry thoughts contribute to anxiety, and discouraging thoughts lead to depression.

Living with a traumatized brain in a traumatized body makes even everyday decisions a challenge and requires the help of your strongest resource, your own inner wisdom. The problem is that intense emotions block access to your inner wisdom. The Wise Mind exercise will help you to access your wise self.

THE WISE MIND

The Wise Mind (Linehan 1993) is the part of our mind where "Emotion Mind" (thoughts based on distressing feelings) and "Reasonable Mind" (rational thoughts) merge together.

Our Wise Mind helps us make sense of our thoughts and feelings, and come up with a balanced response, which satisfies our rational thoughts and also soothes our emotion mind, and, therefore, reduces our distress and helps make us more effective. Whereas the emotion mind wants what it wants when it wants it, the reasonable mind believes you should do what is right. Usually quietly calm, it's that wise inner part of us that just "knows" what is true or valid when we allow ourselves to listen to it.

The wise mind exercise is easily understood using a courtroom analogy. Think of the emotion mind and reasonable mind as lawyers pleading their case to the judge, or wise mind. The judge can't render a verdict until all the evidence has been presented from both sides. Both sides need to be thorough so that the judge has all of the information needed to make the best decision.

An example: You are upset by the way the tennis coach is treating your child. Your child doesn't get to play enough and the coach is tough on her. I should let her quit.

The emotion mind: *The coach is unfair, singling out your child. Your child should quit the team and you should complain to the administration.*

The reasonable mind: *This is your child's first year trying out for the tennis team and, although she is not a strong player yet, she made it! She needs to practice if she wants to get play time. Besides, coaches are tough!*

The Wise Mind response: *Yes, the coach is hard on your child. The coach is tough on everyone on the team. Quitting the team would be unfair to the rest of the team. After all, it is a team sport. The option that is best now is to practice, be patient and support the team from the sidelines.*

EMOTION MIND	WISE MIND	REASONABLE MIND
• *Thinking & behavior controlled by emotional state.*	• *Integrates Emotion Mind & Reasonable Mind.*	• *Intellectual, scientific.*
• *Thoughts are unhelpful & distressing.*	• *Adds intuitive knowing to emotional distress and logical analysis.*	• *Logical and rational thinking.*
• *Difficult to think logically & rationally.*	• *The calm that follows a storm.*	• *Factual thinking, based on evidence.*
• *Facts are distorted to fit with current distress.*	• *Sees or knows something directly & clearly.*	• *Able to plan how to respond.*
• *Emotion drives opinion.*	• *Grasps the bigger picture, rather than just parts.*	• *Focuses attention.*
• *Strong emotions drive strong behavior.*	• *Ensures needs of both Emotional & Reasonable Minds are met: Reasonable Mind is right, but Emotion Mind needs to be soothed.*	• *Cool in approaching problems.*
• **What I want to do.**	• **What are the most appropriate & effective skills that I could use for this situation?**	• **What I should do.**

EXERCISE: Practice the Wise Mind

Think about something that you can't make up your mind about. A decision has to be made but you are concerned about making the right decision.

The issue is:

_____

_____

_____

Using the description of the emotion mind and reasonable mind, List "evidence" in the table provided for each side:

EMOTION MIND	REASONABLE MIND

THE JUDGE'S/ WISE MIND CONCLUSION:

THE IMPACT OVER TIME

"This addiction took my wife away. Why? What was your end game? Ok, so you were acting out. But was making me feel crazy part of your plan?"

~ Sammie, *wounded partner*

The truth is that there is no "end game." A group member recently stated that he now realizes he was in a state of insanity and that his end game was to stay alive. He was shocked by that realization. Justifying their actions to themselves, rationalizing they are not hurting anyone, that "It's just sex," and "I deserve to do whatever I want because I pay all the bills" is a state of insanity! Behavior that involves lying and secrecy and is in violation of one's core moral beliefs is not rational. Every instance of cheating and lying to themselves reinforces all of the negative thoughts and feelings that support the destructive behavior.

Over time, thoughts become beliefs. Repeated infidelity shapes attitudes and beliefs that are increasingly irrational and support terrible destructive behavior. In this state there is no connection between the head and the heart. When that connection is severed, feelings are replaced by a vacant, detached and numb state. At this point manipulation, gaslighting, and deception are the new normal.

This is a disease of the mind. The disease escalates until the deceiver is finally caught. When both partners are working together to rebuild trust, compassion and a program of recovery in earnest, wounds will begin to heal, trust restored, and in most cases, a renewed feeling of intimacy flourishes.

I CONNECTED THE DOTS

"I began to notice that you would avoid telling me things: new shoes, a doctor's appointment, an increase in our electric bill charges. When I was confused about something as minor as the time we were expected at your business dinner, I was made to feel foolish, stupid. There were dozens of instances when you were vague about weekend plans, and when I would ask you again because I had to arrange child care, you would become angry and frustrated, saying, 'I told you last week and again earlier this week.' And then feign concern, saying, 'I'm concerned about your forgetting—maybe you should get checked out.' I now know that you were gaslighting me, purposely being deceptive only to insist that you were communicating clearly and suggesting that I was confused.

"The years and years of lies, deception, shifting blame to me, avoiding conversations, and literally walking away in the middle of a conversation have caused me to doubt myself with everything—do I have a hearing problem? Do I nag? Am I annoying? Do I have early Alzheimers? I lost faith and confidence in myself.

"There were many times that my gut told me there was something wrong. I remember when I went into town for a doctor's appointment, and I thought about surprising you at the office. I took the subway to your office, and when I arrived at my stop, your office, without thinking twice, I remained on the subway. When I got home, I realized that I didn't surprise you that day because my gut told me that something bad would happen if I didn't let you know about my surprise. I probably would have opened your office door and found you having sex on your desk with your secretary or with your pants down, jerking off in front of the computer."

~ Linda, betrayed partner

PAUSE. BREATHE.

> *Self-Care Break*
> ~
>
> Stand up and stretch. Take a slow, mindful walk. As you walk, notice the sensation of your foot as you take each step—heel, ball of foot then toes. Notice the colors around you—the green of leaves and grass, the brown dirt, blue sky. Notice sounds—dog barking, the sounds of traffic, birds chirping. Notice sensations—the breeze on your skin, sun in your eyes. Notice yourself noticing.

EXERCISE: Illustrating Your Thoughts and Feelings

Grab some markers or colored pencils. Think about Linda and Sammie's stories and about your walk. Describe your thoughts and feelings in any way that *doesn't* include words in the space provided here.

HOW DID I GET HERE?

"So much lost time... Weeks of not knowing where you were, what you were doing, where you were going. You refused to deposit your paycheck in our joint account— why? You spent money, moved money around, opened charge cards. Where did the money go? You disclosed that you hid money. Why?

"You betrayed me the whole 30 years of our marriage. You cheated on me with my best friend and maid of honor, my college roommate, and dozens of others. As if that wasn't bad enough, you criticized my parents and my sisters. There were times when the insults became the topic of meals. I began spending time with my mother alone because I didn't want to hear your complaining. You made me feel guilty for wanting to spend time with my family and eroded away at my love for my family. Somehow, I became angry at my family and stopped talking to them. We stopped going to Thanksgiving, birthdays, and other events at my parents' house. I didn't talk to my family for 6 years! I stopped talking to my friends and stopped developing new friendships with school moms because I believed you when you told me I was insecure and too sensitive. YOU LIED TO ME ABOUT YOUR CHEATING AND I BELIEVED EVERY EXCUSE AND WORSE, I BELIEVED THE LIES YOU TOLD ME ABOUT MYSELF!!!

"What was your motive? Why did you remain married to me? Did you ever love me? Did you even like me? Why didn't you divorce me and make life easier on the both of us? Was it a part of your plan to degrade me so that I would put up with anything you said or did? Why did you try to destroy my relationships with my family?"

~ Anita, sad and strong partner

EXERCISE: Feelings Check

Take a feelings check using the SUDS scale. My feeling number is _____ .

Reflect on the stories above.

What stands out for you?

_____

_____

_____

_____

_____

What do you relate to?

_____

_____

_____

_____

Have you had a similar experience? Describe it now.

_____

_____

_____

_____

THERE ARE NO EXCUSES: UNDERSTANDING DESTRUCTIVE ENTITLEMENT

Ivan Boszormenyi-Nagy, psychiatrist and founder of contextual family therapy described entitlement as a right, something earned either through contributions that benefit another or through suffering. For example, an adult abused as a child may develop a sense of constructive entitlement and grow up to become an advocate for abused children. Alternatively, an adult abused as a child may grow up with a chip on their shoulder, believing that "the world owes me." In this sense, destructive entitlement is a type of revenge, "it's *my* turn now" and it overrides guilt and remorse. The person is taking what they deserve. Destructive entitlement fuels wars and leads to divorce.

People struggling with sex addiction live in a state of secret destructive entitlement. There are no reasons that excuse your betrayer's behavior. No amount of childhood abuse or suffering that one endures excuses inflicting harm on those you love the most. Educating yourself about the conditions that led your partner's choices and decisions is an essential component of your healing; *but it is in no way a justification or vindication of egregious behavior*. It is complicated to understand that, for people who struggle with sex addiction, there are two truths: (1) They love their partner (the way they understand love), and (2) They act out sexually with themselves or others. Addiction is, literally, a division of the self. Attitudes, beliefs, and behaviors are in conflict with the whole self. Thinking is disordered. Destructive entitlement in action, selfish and self-centered, they believe they are entitled to a reward for their hard work as a provider. Rob Weiss, CEO of Seeking Integrity and author of *Out of the Doghouse* and *Prodependence* states that people struggling with sex addiction feel entitled to act out and lack the empathy to realize how they have destroyed their partner's trust. Their motto becomes, "*I work hard, I deserve a break.*" Destructive entitlement is a powerful force.

EXERCISE: Daily Journaling

Allow daily journaling to be your frontline resource to navigate through the first year of recovery from betrayal trauma. Although individual therapy is essential for healing, the pain is such that it is like trying to clear sand from a beach one teaspoon at a time. More help is needed to get through each day in the first year. Journaling before or after a distressing event doubles symptom relief. James S. Gordon, M.D., a Harvard educated psychiatrist and founder of The Center for Mind Body Medicine in Washington, D.C., states that scientific research indicates that there is an "inextricable connection among our thoughts, sensations and feelings." Indeed, our mind informs our body. Healthy mind, healthy body.

Your journal is for your eyes only. Find a secure place to store your journal. You will be less likely to access your raw feelings if you do not have a safe place to store your journal. Your thinking mind will edit and control what lands on the page and the part of you that is angry might leave it in a place where your betrayer will find it in an attempt to evoke hurt, shame or empathy.

Approach daily journaling with the intention of reducing your suffering. Trust that this important work will lead you to discover exactly what you need.

Put pen to paper and write whatever comes to mind without trying to direct or edit your writing. Allow whatever is on your mind and in your heart to flow freely onto paper. There is no "right way;" the only rule is to get out of your head and let it flow through the pen.

EXERCISE: My Memories

Pull out your list of relationship memories. Spend time re-reading and adding to the list. Be sure you have included key events in your life, including holidays, vacations, weddings, birth of children, losses, moves, accomplishments, sorrows. Continue to add to the list until it is as complete as possible. You will need it in the chapters ahead.

GOALS

Take a moment to reflect. What do you need right now?

My goal for the day is:

My goal for the week is:

You have faced and slayed the dragon of Reality and you are still standing!

You are ready for the deepest part of your journey, facing your inner self. You are entering the realm of preparing yourself to battle with the monsters and villains of infidelity, facing your own inner foes and, ultimately, transformation of self.

Before you begin, reflect on Donna's wisdom.

"This life as you knew it will be forever changed. Before your body fills with worry know that this isn't necessarily a bad thing. This life of yours could now go in many directions and the best part is that you are now in charge of this! Your relationship with the addict could grow deeper if you decide this is what you now want with everything that has been placed on the table. As scary as it is at this moment, you now get to be in charge of what you can accept for your life and what will not work for you. Please know you didn't cause this and you cannot cure it, repeat this mantra and it will help you!

"It is not fair at all that this person has betrayed you in the most intimate way possible and I am truly sorry for the loss of control that you are now feeling. If you feel the need to endlessly search to make sense of it all like I did, I highly recommend listening to The Four Agreements on audiobook. It will help you to let go of what you cannot control.

"You are a good person and unfortunately bad things happen to good people. Know right now there is NOTHING you could have done to have prevented another person from doing what you now know. Undoubtedly you will replay all of the 'if I had done this' or that 'things would be different,' please know this is not true. You are responsible only for your actions and not the actions of another. When you really get this it will be the beginning of your freedom to your beautiful new life ♥"

~ Donna, compassionate, forgiving and courageous partner

What are you thinking and feeling at this moment? Don't think about it, write it.

CHAPTER 6

REFLECTION

The field of boundless emptiness

Is what exists from the very beginning

You must purify, cure, grind down

Or brush away all the tendencies

You have fabricated into apparent habits

Then you can reside in the

Clear circle of brightness.

~ Hongzhi Zhengjue (1091–1157)

Who are you? Who do you want to be? Betrayal trauma causes a fracture in the foundation of a relationship *and the foundation of self.* The secrets, lies, gaslighting, and deception throughout a relationship is a silent cancer that shatters the infrastructure. The most devastating aspect of discovery is that the entire system collapses into itself. *Your life as you knew it collapsed into itself.* As an example, think about the studio tour at Universal Studios. When the tram approaches the infamous Bates Motel in Alfred Hitchcock's Psycho, it is ominous and haunting. However, when the tram turns the corner, the magic of filmmaking becomes real—the Bates Motel is nothing more than the facade of a building in the front, held up by a pair of two by fours. Norman Bates can no more live in his "Psycho" home than you can live in your pre-discovery home.

The chapter ahead will guide you through the process of reconstructing your life and yourself. To reconstruct, you must grind down, hone, purify, and release to construct a new foundation to build your house upon. In this regard, *your house is your self.*

"It matters not how strait the gate,

How charged with punishments the scroll,

I am the master of my fate,

I am the captain of my soul."

~ William Ernest Henley

WANTS AND NEEDS

Emergency safety needs were established in chapter one. Today, wants and needs become the spackle and nails that hold the walls together. You are in the midst of a life-changing journey. You are gaining strength, resilience and meaning of self. What do you **want** in an intimate partner? If you had a magic wand what would you wish for? Check the qualities that you associate with an intimate partner.

What do you **need**? What is non-negotiable? What is your deal-breaker? Reflect inward and face a deeper truth—what do you refuse to live with. What will you no longer accept in an intimate partner? Circle the qualities that you identify as non-negotiable needs.

LIST OF WANTS AND NEEDS

Companionship	Sex	Loyalty
Support	Respect	Help
Communication	Connection	Security
Affection	Acceptance	Responsibility
Self-care	Listener	Love
Commitment	Fun	Thoughtfulness
Fidelity	Nurturing	Respect
Forgiveness	Accountability	Resilience
Financial Transparency	Tolerance	Kindness
Appreciation	Freedom	Humor
Consideration	Patience	Empathy

Compassion	Trust	Safety
Friendship	Transparency	Honesty
Intimacy	Privacy	Humility
Attentiveness	Forthcoming	Valued
Deferring	Shares Feelings	Reliable
Cherished	Flexible	Beloved

What do you need that is not included on the list?

_____

_____

_____

Are there any roadblocks to getting your needs met?

_____

_____

_____

FACING THE SHADOW SELF

All of us have a shadow side, or part. It is not bad or weak. The shadow is rather what you yourself _perceive_ as dark and weak about yourself, and therefore needs to be hidden and denied. But this depends on your own perspective on life, and your levels of self-esteem. In order to develop a relationship with our shadow part we must listen to it rather than avoid it. Reflect on the roadblocks exercise above. Become ready to accept these difficult feelings into your heart with tenderness. What do you need to let go of? What are you grieving? Are you ready to let go of your anger? Letting go creates space inside. How will you fill that space? What of your life before discovery will you reclaim? When will you be ready to recover positive memories of your life? Imagine yourself becoming ready to find value and appreciation for your betraying partner.

GRIEF, MOURNING AND LETTING GO

Betrayal complicates the process because you are grieving the death of something and someone that is still alive! To move forward, however, we must first move backward. Grief work is necessary to rebuild self. It is an acute reaction that accompanies loss which includes pain and suffering and is unavoidable. Grief allows us to reconnect to our full range of feelings. It disentangles us from the traumatic memories and feelings. Grieving is a process of letting go. It allows for restoration of self, although it may be a self that you haven't seen for a long time.

 EXERCISE: Letting Go

You will need your journal for this exercise.

To aid in the grief process, reflect on the following questions with the intention of letting go. A part of you accepted unacceptable behavior in the past.
Be curious about why.

- Are you worried that letting go implies weakness?

- Are you carrying grudges?

- What is the cost to let them go?

- What did you lose within yourself?

- What was said that you are holding on to?

You are grieving the death of the marriage, your life, as well as the part of you that was living that life.

Is there a part of you that does not want to grieve and let go? A part of you that has a stake in holding on to the painful thoughts and feelings? Ask yourself:

- What am I holding in?

- What am I holding on to? Why do I need to hold on?

In your journal, reflect on the questions above and write about what feelings are coming up for you now that prevent you from letting go.

WHAT I LET GO OF: A BETRAYED PARTNER'S HARMS LIST

(She requested that I read it to my men's recovery group)

"I let go of my own sexuality and in the process much of my femininity. I let go of regular haircuts and new clothes and getting my nails done and getting dressed up

on a Saturday night for my husband, and of hoping he still thinks my aging face and aging body are pretty. I let go of being 'his.' I let go of 'belonging' to someone. I let go of romance and quiet dinners for two and playing footsie and of giving my husband 'the look' that let him know we were going home to share that one thing that was reserved for only him and me. I let go of keeping that part of my marriage alive so that when we were old, we would still have affection and touch and warmth and a deep bond that had been strengthened over the years by mutual self-giving love."

My self—"I am no longer the 'happy' person with the buoyant nature I was for 51 years. Every single day I wind up the new 'me' to get through a day, an hour, a memory, a debilitating trigger that can undo my best efforts in a nanosecond. I look back on who I was and I don't recognize that person anymore. I can no longer discern the murky shadow of my former self on the sidelines of my former life. She no longer beckons me with her memories and hope. She faded into the mist of the relentless fog of my new reality that does not allow for sentimental or wishful thinking. She used to peer into the window of that former life but I can't even see her anymore."

I let go of my vision of what our future was. "The vision I thought we created together when the kids were all sleeping and we would daydream out loud about what life would be like when they were on their own. I let go of planning...vacations, holidays, birthdays and even a Saturday night out with friends. I don't plan on anything anymore other than certain 'uncertainty'. That is my new North Star."

I let go of creativity. "I stopped keeping a pretty house, creating things and trying out new recipes. I let go of dinner parties and changing the sheets and flowers on the table and gardens and summer porch sitting and making Christmas. My creative soul got buried in sorrow and there is no one to help resurrect it."

I let go of what I wanted out of marriage—"I let go of what I got married for. I let go of the idea of a mutually respectful, caring, burden sharing partner. It has been the hardest of all the things to let go of. I had made a God of my husband. He was an idol to me and I adored him in a way that only God Himself deserves to be adored. In letting go I was set adrift with no anchor to stop myself from being tossed and turned on life's seas. I let go of the comfort of someone who knows you and loves you more than they love themselves."

I let go of memories. "I don't recall the happy Christmas' and birthdays and special occasions. When I think of those things now I only wonder to myself about what was happening behind the scenes when I was frosting birthday cakes and looking out the kitchen window waiting for my love to come home. I have no past and no future."

I let go of my pride. "Of my standing in the community, of my ability to walk into a room and not feel like an object of pity and often gossip. I let go of long standing friendships that could not bear the strain of my fragmentation and grief."

I let go of God." He let me down and broke my trust in Him. He led me down what I thought was a garden path. Each day I woke up and started making a home. I went to Mass and offered my day to Him. I was whispering prayers for my husband's safe *return and pleading with God to never take him from me. I was holding him at night as he slept and thanking God through my tears of gratitude for the wonderful husband he gave me. What was God thinking while I was folding laundry and fluffing throw pillows? What was He thinking when my husband was exposing me to the world's diseases? How can I trust a God that did not protect me?"*

I let go of so very much so, please, when I am triggered by any one of these myriad of things that now occupy my once happy mind, please don't ask me to "let it go."

LETTING GO IS A DECISION THAT IS YOURS ALONE TO MAKE. LETTING GO IS A CHOICE AND NOT A MANDATE.

EXERCISE: What I Had to Let Go

Make a list of what you have had to let go:

_____

_____

_____

_____

_____

_____

_____

_____

LETTING GO

In order to let go, you must first revisit and make sense of your life pre-discovery. In her book *Healing Through the Dark Emotions*, Miriam Greenspan states that one must walk straight through the fire to heal. In our twenty-three years working with partners, we can state unequivocally that pain is a necessary part of the process but suffering is not. What happened to you—your discovery—the first moment that you saw what you saw, heard what you heard, with your heart racing and pumping out of your chest and feeling completely detached is a "surreal" experience. Terror and horror and shock vibrated throughout your body. You lived through something that you have never experienced before—ever—and it was terrifying! You felt that your life had suddenly been murdered and yet, there are no bodies or blood or ambulances, no EMT's, ER's, earthquakes, tornados, category 4 hurricanes, tsunamis or emergency alerts. As you know, this life-threatening moment is the real experience. It's the collision of what you learned with what you felt emotionally as well as felt in your body and, for many, the flood of thoughts that made you more terrified.

Sex addiction–induced betrayal trauma is your tsunami, 9.0 earthquake, explosion, 9/11. It happened in your safe haven, your comfort zone. It isn't what happened in that worst moment that caused post-traumatic stress disorder, it is all that unfolded afterwards; it is the sense you begin to make of what happened to you that results in extreme, and for many, acute symptoms.

 EXERCISE: Grief and Mourning

You will need your journal for this exercise. Write a grief and mourning letter. Consider writing more than one letter. Will you write a letter to your betrayer? Yourself? Use the sentence prompts as a guide. *The letter is for your eyes only.*

Dear_____,

I hate it when...

It makes (made) me furious when...

I'm tired of...

I can no longer accept when...

It hurts when...

I feel sad when...

I feel awful when...

I feel disappointment when...

I feel betrayed when...

I feel dismissed when...

I feel unimportant when...

I feel invisible when...

I'm afraid that...

I feel scared that...

I feel puzzled by...

I am afraid that...

I am worried that...

I feel shame about...

I feel guilt about...

I regret that...

I blame myself for...

I need you to...

I want for you to...

I expect you to...

CHAPTER 7

FORGIVENESS *vs.* UNFORGIVENESS

"Without forgiveness, there can be no compassion."

~ Thich Nhat Hanh

"I think the first step is to understand that forgiveness does not exonerate the abuser. Forgiveness liberates the victim. It is a gift you give yourself."

~ T.D. Jakes

In 2006, the Amish community of Nickel Mines, Pennsylvania, taught our nation about forgiveness. On October 2, 2006, Charles Roberts, a local non–Amish neighbor, entered an Amish schoolhouse and shot ten Amish girls between the ages of six and fourteen. He killed five girls and then took his own life. The world was shocked to learn that a group of Amish people, some of whom lost their child only a few hours earlier, went to Charles Roberts' home to express forgiveness to his wife. Later, another group of Amish people went to Charles Roberts' parents' house to express forgiveness and offer support. An Amish man held Mr. Roberts' father for one hour while he cried. The Amish attended Charles Roberts' funeral and arranged that monies were given as gifts to Charles Roberts' family.

Three years earlier, in May of 2003, a conference was held in Switzerland called "Heal our Land." As part of the 16th-century church reformation, Swiss pastors tortured, beheaded, burned, and drowned Anabaptists, or Amish, to death because they were unwilling to be baptized in Switzerland's reformed church. Modern-day Swiss Christians, they believed, were "cursed" by the crimes of their ancestors. Anabaptists, having fled Switzerland by 1550, settled in Lancaster County, PA.

Swiss pastors felt compelled to acknowledge the atrocities of their brethren. The pastors invited the Amish and Mennonites (also Anabaptists) of Lancaster County to travel to Switzerland. They acknowledged wrongs done to the Anabaptists and asked for forgiveness. Thirty reformed pastors, dressed in their clerical robes, publicly washed the feet of every Anabaptist person that attended. The same pastors knelt on stage before the American Mennonite and Amish leaders. With tears, the same pastors asked for verbal affirmation of forgiveness from every leader and their wives. The Amish and Mennonites granted forgiveness. Later, a government official publicly asked for forgiveness on behalf of the government for the persecutions against the Anabaptists.

Shortly after that, Amish leaders went on to ask forgiveness of the Mennonite community for judging and thus creating division among the groups. The Mennonite leaders and government officials went on to apologize for historical wrongs and indifference committed against the Native American tribes that owned the land they settled upon arriving in Lancaster County.

Their official "Acknowledgment and Apology to Native Peoples" noted historical wrongs, including:

- Dishonest actions by the government and military.

- Social injustices and prejudices by immigrant peoples.

- Sins of those bearing the name of Christ.

The apology referenced a massacre of American Indians, referred to as "one of the great scandals in American history."

Amish and Mennonite leaders stated that "The complicit condoning by the Pennsylvania government of massacres set the tone for the way the U.S. eventually settled the West. As a Christian, I not only apologize, I ask for forgiveness." Amish and Mennonites reconciled with their indigenous neighbors.

Amish and Mennonite leaders then embarked upon a repentance mission to Israel in 2010. A draft of a *Declaration of Repentance* was presented to the Nation of Israel by the Anabaptist Nation. Anabaptists humbly sought forgiveness from the Jewish people for having ignored their persecution throughout Europe for over two centuries. They admitted that the Anabaptist Nation as a whole had cursed the nation of Israel by choosing to remain indifferent and collectively silent, most regrettably so during the Nazi Holocaust.

The Swiss pastors knew that the inherited shame was a blight on current and future generations. They realized that time in and of itself does not heal. The Swiss and Anabaptists realized that true healing in relationships comes through forgiveness as modeled in their religious texts.

In 1994, Nelson Mandela was elected to government formally ending Apartheid in South Africa. Healing the atrocities of Apartheid was necessary for the nation to move ahead. Archbishop Desmond Tutu led the Truth and Reconciliation Commission. Reparations to victims and their families began a multi-generational healing process. An essential part of healing is for victims to tell their stories. The Truth and Reconciliation Commission compiled a full, objective, and comprehensive record of the effects of Apartheid on South African society. Anyone who was a victim of violence was welcome to give their testimony before this newly-constituted body. Perpetrators of violence could also provide evidence and request amnesty from prosecution. The perpetrators of violence committed moral injuries against themselves. They needed self-forgiveness to be healthy and contribute to the healing of others. Telling their story, and being recorded into South African history, allowed the perpetrators to heal. The Commission understood that "To forgive is not just to be altruistic, [but] it is the best form of self-interest." The Mandela government acknowledged that "To err is human; to forgive, divine" (www.sahistory.com).

The German government, committed to the healing of their nation, maintains concentration and extermination camps Auschwitz-Birkenau, Bergen-Belsen, Buchenwald, Dachau, among many other Holocaust memorials. The healing of ancestors of victims and perpetrators depends upon "never forgetting."

After the 1994 genocide in Rwanda, murderers were released from prison if they were willing to seek forgiveness and offer restitution. Murderers sought forgiveness from the families of the people they murdered. They offered restitution through rebuilding homes, planting and harvesting crops. The murderers returned to the communities where they lived. They killed their lifelong friends and neighbors with machetes—often with their children witnessing their gruesome murder. Through these consistent and humble actions, victims and murderers are healing. A village leader states that "Seeking forgiveness from a family where you killed relatives is an act of courage."

EXERCISE: Defining Forgiveness

What does forgiveness mean to me?

_____

_____

_____

_____

_____

_____

Does any part of you hear that you are being asked to forgive your betrayer? If so, go back and re-read the chapter. It is important to pause when emotions are high because people don't always hear clearly under stressful conditions.

"It's easier to forgive an enemy than to forgive a friend."

~ William Blake

THE LESSON

The lessons of healing unforgivable harm are not lost on us. The nature of the violation is of little consequence in healing. Regardless of the offense, the impact on the victim is the same. Shock, fear, and horror lead to unrelenting pain. In betrayal trauma, the harm is profound because it is personal. The violation occurred from an enemy within. The safety of your home, family, and heart was breached by the person you trusted without reservation. The hurt is profound.

Healing of the mind, heart, and soul must happen at the same time that you are angry and enraged. Hurt that is unresolved over time becomes anger. In betrayal trauma, unrelenting fearful thoughts (What else is he capable of?) increase anxiety exponentially. Obsessive fearful thoughts stoke the flame of anger. Without a healing/recovery process, anger intensifies. Injustice is born of toxic anger. Injustice becomes a dangerous "call to action," leading to acts of revenge. The belief that "people" have been wronged fertilize the seeds of war. Retribution is the battle call— the "solution." The ongoing wars, conflicts, and bombings between Arabs and Jews and past conflicts between Northern Ireland (Brits and Scots) and Ireland's indigenous Irish, Hutu's and Tutsi's of Rwanda, among others, are salient examples of the cost to humanity of toxic, unrelenting anger and unforgiveness.

"To forgive is to set a prisoner free and discover that the prisoner was you."

~ Lewis B. Smedes

FORGIVENESS IS NOT:

- Forgetting.
- Weakness.
- Giving up the right to be angry.
- A "get out of jail free" card.
- An invitation to have sex.
- A level playing field.
- An expectation.
- A couples journey.
- Taking the easy way out.
- A pass.
- Passive resignation.
- Easy.
- A message that you have moved on.
- Related to religious beliefs.
- Required for relationship healing.
- A mandate.
- Giving up or giving in.
- A reason for the betrayer to issue a list of complaints.

The purpose of forgiveness is to free your heart from the barbed wire that is wrapped around it.

 EXERCISE: Forgive Who?

MAKE A LIST OF PEOPLE YOU NEED TO FORGIVE.	MAKE A LIST OF PEOPLE YOU WOULD LIKE TO BE FORGIVEN BY.	MAKE A LIST OF WHAT YOU NEED TO FORGIVE YOURSELF FOR.

FORGIVENESS IS:

- Never forgetting.
- Taking control of one's life.
- Releasing stress.
- Victory
- Reclaiming dignity.
- Strength.
- Transformative.
- Giving up the need for revenge.
- Honoring self.
- Maintaining physical health.
- Supporting your Mental health.
- Courageous.
- Open-hearted.
- Acceptance of past.
- Self-leadership (*being the captain of my ship*).
- **FREEDOM.**

THE PATH OF FORGIVENESS

In *The Book of Forgiving*, Desmond and Mpho Tutu describe the fourfold path of forgiveness; telling the story, naming the hurt, granting forgiveness, and renewing or releasing the relationship.

Psychotherapist and former monk, Thomas Moore, believes that forgiveness appears in its own time and in its own way and that "we create the conditions in which it will appear."

Reverend James Forbes, whose ancestors were slaves, stated, "I am a black man. If I should spend all of my time talking about slavery and what the oppressors did, I guarantee I would not have the quality of life that I ought to live." Offenses are never adequately atoned. It is not healthy to maintain vigilance in anger and revenge—the soul longs for peace.

Anger lights up the pleasure pathways in the brain. When we decide to act on our anger to "make them pay," our brain rewards us by releasing neurochemicals that stoke the flames of anger. It's the same process as an addiction—the pleasure center in the brain is activated. Holding on to grudges is harmful, and forgiveness is good for health. Anger increases the heart rate and is connected to the fight/flight response. According to Harvard Medical School, anger can trigger a heart attack.

THE BELIEF THAT THE DECEIVER NEEDS TO APOLOGIZE IN ORDER FOR YOU TO FORGIVE IS A MYTH.

Forgiveness is not forgetting. Forgiveness is not condoning bad behavior. **When you forgive, you are not saying that what the person did was acceptable**. You are merely stating that what they did was not acceptable. The violation happened, and you cannot change it. You will remember the incident(s), but there is no need to carry around the anger for the rest of your life.

Forgiveness is a process of opting out of anger and the need for revenge—forgiving the human qualities that lead people to act in terrible ways.

Forgiveness is a decision.

Lynn MGinn, who lost her husband in 9/11, states, "I would like to move on from— 'I've been wronged'—and I need to embrace another idea instead of anger, hate, revenge, bitterness, war, bias, and prejudice."

Holocaust survivor, Elie Wiesel, states that there are two types of forgiveness in Jewish tradition—to God and your fellow man. God can forgive a transgression against God but cannot forgive a transgression toward a fellow man. That is between fellow men.

EXERCISE: Connecting to Your Wise Self

Take a few minutes to connect to your wise self. How are you feeling? Where in your body are you feeling any sensation or energy right now? What are you thinking? If you are sensing fear remind yourself that there is no danger and that you are safe.

_____

_____

_____

_____

PAUSE. BREATHE.

WHAT SPIRITUAL LEADERS HAVE TO SAY ABOUT FORGIVENESS

"You must forgive those who hurt you, even if whatever they did to you is unforgivable in your mind. You will forgive them not because they deserve to be forgiven, but because you don't want to suffer and hurt yourself every time you remember what they did to you. Forgiveness is your own mental healing.

"Forgiveness is an act of self-love."

~ Don Miguel Ruiz

"Loving yourself means accepting yourself, including your past. We all make mistakes, and we all have regrets, but there's no reason to carry those mistakes with us until the end of our lives."

~ Eleanor Roosevelt

"No one can make you feel inferior without your consent."

~ Eleanor Roosevelt

"Watch your thoughts, they become your words; watch your words, they become your actions; watch your actions, they become your habits; watch your habits, they become your character; watch your character, it becomes your destiny."

~ Lao Tzu

"Forgiveness doesn't excuse their behavior. Forgiveness prevents their behavior from destroying your heart."

~ Unknown

"If we really want to love we must learn how to forgive."

~ Mother Teresa

"To forgive is the highest, most beautiful form of love. In return, you will receive untold peace and happiness."

~ Robert Muller

"Forgiving does not erase the bitter past. A healed memory is not a deleted memory. Instead, forgiving what we cannot forget creates a new way to remember. We change the memory of our past into a hope for our future."

~ Lewis B. Smedes

"Without storms, there would be no rainbows."

~ Terry Roberts, mother of Charles Roberts, shooter at Nickel Mines elementary school

"Forgive those who didn't love you. They were teaching you how to love yourself."

~ Ryan Elliot

WHY IT IS IMPORTANT TO FORGIVE

Because no one who truly forgives can continue to suffer. Whoever forgives is healed. You release yourself from illusions of perfection. At the same time, those who hold on to resentment and anger bind themselves to it.

Forgiveness undoes what fear has produced. Forgiveness is the great release from living in the past as if it is the present. For what has healed, no longer is.

The unforgiving mind is torn with doubt. It is confused about all it sees, is afraid and angry, weak and blustering, scared to go ahead, afraid to stay, afraid to awaken or to go to sleep, fearful of every sound, yet more fearful of stillness, terrified of darkness, yet more terrified at the approach of light.

FORGIVENESS IS AN ACTION, NOT A FEELING

"We are all things. We are the cage, we are the key to the cage and the freedom that lies beyond it."

~ Lee Neale

You cannot feel forgiveness until you do it. Many people say, "I can't forgive because I don't feel it." Of course not. You cannot feel something you haven't experienced. The feeling can only come when you verbalize forgiveness within yourself. Take action first—verbalize—then feeling follows.

EXERCISE: Contemplating Forgiveness

What do I think about forgiveness?

_____

_____

_____

What do I feel when I contemplate forgiveness?

_____

_____

_____

What do I believe that I can't forgive? In myself? Who else?

_____

_____

_____

What is unforgivable?

_____

_____

_____

What do I need to release myself from unforgiveness?

_____

_____

_____

Forgiving ourselves for all our past harms to others and ourselves would enable us to be compassionate with others. Self-forgiveness is accepting yourself as a human being who has faults and makes mistakes. You no longer need to carry sorrow and regret over a self-inflicted personal offense. Give yourself the gift of self-love and calm your heart from self-rejection, thoughts of failure, and the burden of guilt. Let go of the need to work hard to make up for past offenses.

The process of practicing forgiveness is not based in logic. It must be based on faith. The betrayal is so profound as to require a more elevated means to forgive. We are limited in our ability to forgive intellectually and emotionally. It is a spiritual endeavor. Those who can achieve deep forgiveness often have a faith-based belief that they can draw upon for support. For many, the need to elevate to a higher level is essential to ensure a place in the world to come. In many religious practices, atonement is a part of spiritual practice. In the Jewish tradition, the High Holiday of Yom Kippur, the Day of Atonement, is a period of reflection and seeking atonement, or forgiveness, from friends and family, then for self, and then from God *as you understand him.* In Christianity, Easter (and for Catholics Lent) is a period of humbly seeking repentance for sins from God.

In her book *Radical Forgiveness*, Tara Brach, Ph.D. states that those who are "unable to get past rage, sadness, and grief are controlled by the need for revenge...[one] cannot escape the prison of their own victimhood."

Dr. Brach goes on to say that we can transform a hurt when we do so at a spiritual level as a "mission." It will not change what happened to you—nothing can do that—but it will change how you experience the wound.

In the movie *Dead Man Walking*, a nun helps a murderer on death row to find salvation through accepting responsibility for taking innocent lives. He found humility and peace in repentance. He was able to seek and receive forgiveness. When he was put to death, feeling his humanity, he begged forgiveness of the victims' families.

You may be thinking, the above examples are all well and good, but my pain is much deeper and more personal. Just keep in mind forgiving *is* possible. It does not happen easily or quickly. Forgiveness is an endeavor to extricate yourself from the pain connected to what happened to you. It allows freedom from the throbbing pain and unrelenting sorrow.

Forgiveness is a continual action. It occurs with a thought, a moment of grace, or as a result of apologies. Forgiveness is a continual journey of the heart.

BATTLING THE FORGIVENESS BOGEYMAN

We cannot forgive and get past what we refuse to remember. We cannot heal if we refuse to release anger. The adage "forgive and forget" may be possible with small offenses. Betrayal trauma is not a minor offense. "Time heals all wounds" does not pertain to betrayal trauma. The wound worsens over time if not healed. With harm as profound as a betrayal, forgetting is dangerous. If we do not allow ourselves to "feel the pain" and "learn the lesson," it might happen again. The first step to forgiving is remembering.

Remembering is painful. It is essential to take good care of yourself now. Go slowly. Prepare yourself for an internal struggle. There may be a part of you that avoids remembering because "it's in the past."

Mindfulness Breath Break

~

Stop. Place your hand on your stomach—the area above your belly button and below your diaphragm. Keep your shoulders still. Inhale a long and slow breath in *through your nose*, feeling your hand move out. The breath will pull your diaphragm down and push your belly out. Feel your hand move out with your gut. Exhale *through your mouth* slowly. Feel your stomach and your hand move in.

In *The Book of Forgiving*, Desmond and Mpho Tutu state, "*We are not responsible for what breaks us, but we can be responsible for what puts us back together again.*" Identifying our hurts enables us to repair our broken parts and reclaim our true selves.

EXERCISE: The Big Hurts

Identify the deepest hurt. List your feelings. Using the feeling list in the appendix, turn inward and be exhaustive in your search. Remember that injuries are real, even if they don't leave a visible bruise. You cannot heal feelings that you don't own!

Identify the hurts that you are ready to release.

EXERCISE: Your Story, (Again)

Reflect on forgiveness and how it applies to you. Use what you have learned about yourself to shape your perspective. Write the story of what happened to you again. Begin at the beginning of your story. Speak your story aloud. If you have a friend, sponsor, therapist, or other trusted person, read them the story. If not, read it aloud to yourself, while facing a mirror. You must tell YOUR story to heal.

CHAPTER 8

RELEASE AND RECONSTRUCTION

After the discovery of your beloved's infidelity and deception, you accepted the call to action. That call has taken you on a journey inward—which is nothing less than a heroes' journey. This journey has required courage, loyalty and temperance. You have faced the two-headed monster of disclosure, slain your own inner dragons, faced unknown creatures and, ultimately, met parts of yourself that have been operating below the surface in ways that have kept you in pain. Each phase of your journey has been a grinding down, shedding, and brushing away of unhealthy attitudes, beliefs and behaviors that threaten your mind, body, and spirit. Your heroes' journey has brought you to this moment of letting go in order to receive.

You are ready for the final challenge to complete this stage of your transformational process. Ahead, you will reflect on the discoveries you have made on your journey, what has been lost, what must be let go to make space for the new, and what the meaning of this journey is for you.

THE DARK NIGHT OF THE SOUL

Eckart Tolle describes the dark night of the soul as a collapse of the perceived meaning of life; the meaning you gave to your life. The discovery of infidelity, deception and trickery by your beloved caused a shattering of all that defined your life—your accomplishments, activities, everything that you considered important was invalidated.

At the bottom of the abyss is salvation; the blackest moment is the moment where transformation begins; It is always darkest before the dawn. Through the lens of greek mythology, betrayed partners are the Phoenix. The Phoenix flies toward the sun to be burned to ashes and then, to be born again. They know that the only way to heal is to head straight into the fire. The exercises ahead will move you through the process of putting to rest who you knew yourself to be.

EXERCISE: Dark Night of the Soul

What does a "darkest moment" mean to you?

_____

_____

_____

_____

_____

Describe your darkest moment. Continue in your journal if you run out of room.

What was taken from you that set you out on this journey?

Reflect on your life before discovery; the life you know in your heart that you cannot return to. What has been the hardest to let go?

Make an exhaustive list of *everything* from your life before discovery that you now realize you need to let go. Use your journal if you run out of space.

What are the burdens placed upon you by your betrayer that you are ready to release?

What burdens have you taken on?

Is there a part of you that needs to hold on to a "victimized" role? Is this part ready to take a victor role?

What do you need in order to be able to release yourself from the bondage of the burdens put upon you by your betrayer's actions?

Are you able to commit to yourself that you will get your need met in the next 3 days?

 EXERCISE: Draw the Final Battle

You will need an 8 1/2 x 11 piece of paper and markers, pastels or colored pencils. In spirit of the biblical story of Jonah and the great fish, for a moment, imagine that you are Jonah and you are in the belly of the whale; or imagine that you are Darth Vader in battle with Obi-Wan Kanobie; or Simba in his battle with Scar, the Lion King's murderer; or The Avengers in battle with Thanos; or Harry Potter and Lord Voldemort; or David and Goliath; or Batman and the Joker. You are in the darkest part of the battle. Are you battling monsters of stuckness? An obsessive mind? A thief of your spirituality? Anger? Fear? Depression? Surrender? Draw your battle. Are the monsters wearing battle masks? Draw the scene that depicts the battle and your victory. Share your battle story with your therapist.

EXERCISE: Getting Ready

If I release my need to control my partner's recovery, that would mean...

_____

_____

_____

If I release my feelings of being trapped in a victimized role and accept my survivor role, that would mean...

_____

_____

_____

What is getting in the way of releasing negative feelings from my trauma story?

_____

_____

_____

Are there any hurt, resentful or angry parts inside that need something in order to let go? Any needs that have not been spoken or met?

_____

_____

_____

Write a statement committing to meet needs that stand in the way of letting go of pain. Begin the statement with:

Even though I risk _____ *, I commit to* _____

_____

_____

_____

For me, releasing means...

_____

_____

_____

Accepting that I am where I am supposed to be at this time in my life suggests...

_____

_____

_____

_____

_____

_____

_____

_____

EXERCISE: Forgiveness Letter

Write a forgiveness letter to yourself. Include everything you would wish to hear from someone from whom you seek forgiveness. Include everything on your mind and in your heart; judgements, resentments, guilt. Acknowledge that you are responsible for your thoughts, feelings and actions going forward. Acknowledge the reality that there is a good reason you remain in the relationship for today. Compliment yourself for your courage and for seeking help. State what you intend to do to make things as right for yourself as possible. Apologize to yourself for holding onto grudges and guilt that cause you harm.

PREPARATION FOR THE RELEASE CEREMONY:
GATHERING UP, REFLECT AND RESPECT, RECLAIM AND RECONSTRUCT

A ceremony is a ritual of connection, or a coming together. Marriages, Bar Mitzvah's, confirmations, tributes, religious holidays unite communities. They honor self-worth, identity, life's purpose, and social connection to others and values. Ceremonies mark significant changes such as marriages, funerals, retirement, children leaving home and other meaningful milestones. A ceremony is a sacred experience. Set time aside to create an experience that is deeply significant and that you can approach with an open, loving heart. This moment is irreplaceable What does this ceremony symbolize for you?

As you enter the process of release and the final stages of physical, emotional and spiritual transformation, state aloud the ceremony you are beginning. Betrayed partners often refer to their ceremonies as a letting go, releasing, reclaiming, cleansing, honoring, goddess, hero, or heroine ceremony.

GATHERING UP

Gather together and make a photocopy of all of the exercises throughout the workbook that brought you to this moment. You may choose to make a copy of all of the exercises or those that were particularly meaningful. Through the release process, the copies will be destroyed so be sure to use copies only. Although you may want to destroy the original exercise, I encourage you to use copies. There may be a time in the future that you will want to revisit this experience—although that may seem unlikely today. Make an agreement with yourself that, at this time, you will use copies knowing that you can always destroy the originals in the future.

Include journal entries that contain sensitive, painful thoughts and feelings. Include anything in your unhelpful thought box. Include the metaphors and analogies that resonated with your story. Don't include your affirmations, gratitudes, or any other exercises that support your healing.

REFLECT AND RESPECT

Reread the stories that you wrote during your healing process. Notice the way your story shifted through your heroes' journey. Take time to *be* with it all; from the darkest and most frightening moments; through the confusion, distress, and fear; through the perils encountered along the way; memories revisited; sadness and grief; anger and shame; forgiveness and acceptance; to strength and victory. Before moving on, offer respect, kindness, and compassion to the one inside who suffered and broke apart. Perhaps you would like to commit to the most tender parts of yourself that you will always be tuned inward and listen to.

Offer yourself gratitude. You have brought the inner darkness into the light.

PREPARE THE SITE

For this experience, you will need fire **if you can use fire safely**. Fire symbolizes purification, wisdom, knowledge, and passion, strengths needed to build your heroes' house. You will be releasing the past, the hurts, and suffering, negative thoughts, and feelings, resentments, grudges, regrets. You are making space to construct a stronger, sturdier, you; broken and yet, no worse for the wear. Grinding, down, shedding, casting off, unburdening, letting go.

A fireplace, fire-pit, Chiminea, a metal trash can, or a stockpot with a lid will work well. Be sure to have a fire extinguisher nearby. If fire doesn't work, use water.

You will need your photocopied exercises. Include any mementos, **copies** of photos, flowers, or anything else that you sense needs to be included in this release.

Choose a place that is secure and private for your release ceremony. Ceremonies often begin with a statement of intention, action, and closure.

PREPARE YOURSELF

Approach the process mindfully. Think about what you will wear. People generally wear black to funerals and tuxedos for formal events. As you begin the ceremonial process, pay attention to your senses; what do you see? Smell? Hear? Feel? Where do you feel it in your body? Notice how connected you feel inside. Following is one suggestion for conducting your ceremony. Remember that it is *your* ceremony. Include elements that are important to you.

PAUSE. BREATHE.

> *Mindfulness Breath Break*
>
> ~
>
> Take a moment to close your eyes, inhale for four counts, taking the breath all the way down to your diaphragm and then exhale for eight counts out your mouth. Repeat five times. Open your eyes and notice the sensation of calm inside.

Check in with yourself. Are you feeling angry? Release the anger now by writing, stomping your feet, screaming, or whatever works for you. You don't want to begin a fire ceremony in the "heat" of the moment.

 EXERCISE: The Release Ceremonies

1. Begin by preparing the fire. In the spirit of mindfulness, acknowledge the fire. It is a part of your release ceremony.

2. What do you want to get out of your experience? Set your intention (*I will let go with grace or I will stay in a relaxed body*). Make a declarative statement, "*I am releasing the burdens of betrayal trauma.*"

3. Readings (See appendix for examples).

4. Gather up all that you brought with you. Lay it out on the floor and sit with it—just be with it. Every item you have before you was a part of your heroes' journey; the good, the bad, and the ugly. You lived and experienced every bit of what is in front of you. The items are a proxy for all that you have been through. You are releasing your burdens of suffering, not your story.

5.   Before each item is placed in the fire, make the following statement aloud; "*I now release the hold that*_____ *(feelings/beliefs) has had on me.*"

6.   When all of the items have been placed in the fire, acknowledge aloud that the fire (or water) has cleansed your heart, opening it to receive love.

7.   Do you want to dance around the fire? Dancing around the fire symbolizes and celebrates the cleansing power of fire. The phoenix burns in order to rise from its ashes.

8.   If it feels right to read the Native American prayer aloud, do so now. If a different prayer feels right, recite it aloud.
     (Additional prayers are in the appendix)

We return thanks to our mother,

the earth, which sustains us.

We return thanks to the rivers and streams

which supply us with water.

We return thanks to all herbs, which furnish medicines

for the cure of our diseases.

We return thanks to the corn, and to her sisters,

the beans and squashes, which give us life.

We return thanks to the bushes and trees,

which provide us with fruit.

We return thanks to the wind,

which, moving the air, has banished diseases.

We return thanks to the moon and the stars,

which have given us their light when the sun was gone.

We return thanks to our grandfather He-no,

that he has protected his grandchildren from witches and reptiles,

and has given us his rain.

We return thanks to the sun,

that he has looked upon the earth with a beneficent eye.

Lastly, we return thanks to the Great Spirit,

in whom is embodied all goodness,

and who directs all things for the good of his children.

~ Iroquois traditional

"Forgiveness is an act of the will, and the will can function regardless of the temperature of the heart."

~ Corrie Ten Boom

PREPARE YOUR HEART

A successful forgiveness release requires that you are free of negative and burdensome emotions. Before you begin, place your hands on your heart. Feel and listen. Do all of you feel serene, calm and at peace? Use breath breaks and your trauma toolkit to restore harmony within. The pain of anger and resentment reside in the heart, so, the intention of **forgiveness releases your imprisoned heart.**

For your ceremony, gather photocopies of your forgiveness exercises in chapters seven and eight. Look through your journal and exercises throughout the book for areas that focus on forgiveness. Add any items that represent thoughts, feelings, attitudes, and behaviors that keep you stuck in a state of unforgiveness toward yourself or anyone else.

In preparation for the event:

- List three declarative statements that represent your intention. For example:

  - *"Today I release anger from my heart."*

  - *"I will no longer believe that I am not enough."*

- Make a list of what you will forgive yourself for in the ceremony.

- Make a list of all judgmental thoughts you have toward yourself and others.

- Make a list of who you need to forgive and what needs to be forgiven in the ceremony. Choose three affirmations that will replace the negative thoughts and beliefs about yourself. For example:

  - *"I am loveable just as I am."*

  - *"I can accept my reality and I can choose my reality."*

  - *"I am responsible for my own happiness."*

  - *"I can let go of anger today."*

- There is more than one truth in all relationships. Using the list of those who you will be offering forgiveness for, make a list of what worked; what was good and brought meaning to you at the time.

- Forgiveness follows grief and mourning. Include exercises in your workbook and journal that focus on grief and loss.

EXERCISE: The Forgiveness Ceremony

To conduct the ceremony you will need a quiet and private space, the items that you will release including the photocopies of forgiveness exercises, any objects that represent the process, and two chairs.

1. Begin the ceremony with your declarative statements, setting the intention of the process. Request help from any source that works for you (religious, spiritual or any other source from which you draw peace). Ask that your source(s) are present with you to witness your release and to offer nurturing, compassion and acceptance.

2. Read any prayers, inspirations, statements or anything else that is fitting for the process.

3. Arrange the chairs so that they are facing one another.

4. Put the part of you that you are offering forgiveness to in the chair. Parts that you may invite to sit in the chair include, the "victim" part, the angry part, the shameful part, the caregiver, the helpless part, the abusive part, the peacemaker part, the resentful part, the needy part, the grudge holder and any other parts that feel right.

5. With gentleness, compassion and an open heart, read your exercises, lists, writings, and anything else that pertains to forgiveness of yourself, sitting in the chair. At the point that feels right to you, state aloud to the part:

    "I no longer hold you responsible for _____ .

    I release you from _____ . *You no longer need to* _____ ."

6. Read the letter of forgiveness that you wrote to yourself.

7. Make a commitment, aloud, to choose to remain in a forgiving state to maintain inner peace and an open and compassionate heart.

 EXERCISE: Review Your Burdens

Reflect on the burdens that you have been carrying in your relationship—before and after discovery. Have you been keeping his secret? Have you been making excuses for his withdrawal, temper, isolation, disconnection? Do you carry burdens about yourself as a result of his behavior—overweight, appearance, sex too soon after childbirth, mood, nagging. The burden of his shame. Make a list of each burden you are carrying as a result of discovery of your SA's behavior. Next to each burden, list how the burden has affected you.

THE BURDEN	ITS EFFECT ON ME
Chaos.	I feel stupid because I can't remember things.
No choice.	I am invisible.
Financial fear.	Worry, checking bank accounts.

Examples

Get a pile of cloths, towels, whatever you have handy. Get a pile of books; the bigger the better. Choose a cloth for each burden you identify. Choose a book to represent the effect the burden has had on you (illness, sleep loss). Place two chairs opposite of one another. Choose a cloth to represent your betrayer. Put a cloth on the chair that your betrayer will sit in. Sit across from your betrayer.

Knowing that these burdens are not yours and that they were given to you to carry upon discovery, you will give the burdens back to your betrayer. You have been betrayed. You have been victimized. You are carrying the burden of the harm and pain and the difficult decisions you make daily. You cannot heal your own wound when you are carrying his burdens. It is time to give them back.

Sitting across from your betrayer, pick up each cloth, one at a time saying

"I have been carrying the burden of _____ since _____ . This burden is not mine. It is not of my own doing. I will no longer carry the burden of _____ . I am giving it back to you."

Put the cloth on your betrayer's chair. Continue this process until complete. You will do the same with each book, saying:

"The burden of _____ has caused me to _____ (loose sleep, become depressed) and is affecting my wellbeing. I will no longer carry the burden of _____ . I am giving it to you to carry.

Now that you have given the burdens back, what are you willing to do to take care of yourself in the future?

State the commitment to take care of yourself aloud.

State aloud how it feels to have given the burdens back.

Check inward and notice any lingering resentments—get rid of them now by stating:

"I am releasing my resentment to _____ for _____.

Reflect on how your suffering through this horrible trauma made you stronger. You may not have all of the answers & information you need, but your closure will come from continuing to release resentments (aloud) and offering yourself forgiveness every day.

Take a moment to reflect on your experience. You have released all of the thoughts, beliefs, feelings, and behaviors that were keeping your "house" damaged and preventing you from moving forward. Are you ready to build your new house? Take a deep break and move forward.

RECONSTRUCTION—USING THE BUILDING OF A HOUSE AS AN ANALOGY FOR BUILDING YOUR "INNER HOUSE"

There are ten steps to building your heroes' house: (1) Have a solid blueprint; (2) Prepare the land; (3) Lay the foundation; (4) Frame it out; (5) Install plumbing, electrical, and HVAC; (6) Install insulation; (7) Hang up drywall; (8) Finish the exterior; (9) Secure the fixtures and flooring; and (10) Complete an inspection and final walk-through.

EXERCISE: Building Your Heroes' House

As the architect of your house, what do you need in order to attribute all that you associate with trustworthiness to yourself? Is anger, embarrassment, helplessness, forgiveness toward yourself blocking you from fully trusting yourself? List the roadblocks to trusting yourself and why:

ANGER	HELPLESSNESS	FORGIVENESS	EMBARRASSMENT
I'm so stupid. Why would I do this to myself?	*I've never had to make major decisions—what if I make a mistake?*	*I let myself believe the lies. I chose to stick my head in the sand.*	*What's wrong with me that I would stay with someone who did this to me?*

Examples

PREPARING THE LAND (ASSESSING READINESS)

Before pouring the foundation, the land needs to be cleared of rocks and debris. Any rubble, trash, or other traces of wreckage must be cleared. You can't build a solid house on shakey ground.

  1. Close your eyes and focus on your inner world of thoughts and feelings. Is my heart intact? What needs to be cleared?

_____

_____

_____

2. Make a list of anything more that needs to be released? Is there loose debris? Include knowledge, images, anything that is now working against your healing.

_____

_____

_____

  3. Are there any negative thoughts and feelings remaining toward your betrayer that need to be released?

_____

_____

_____

LAYING THE FOUNDATION

The villains confronted in the crisis phase of your heroes' journey have been defeated. There will be new villains ahead; keep your crisis toolkit nearby. The ground is cleared and it is time to construct your essential toolkit. This toolkit will become a normal part of your everyday life, keeping you steady and balanced.

My Essential Toolkit includes:

1. My palm stone	2. My affirmations	3.
4.	5.	6.
7.	8.	9.

FRAMING IT OUT

The concrete and steel rods that are designed to withstand earthquakes, storms, tornados are ready to be installed. Continue to monitor your inner world for cracks.

The skeleton of your heroes' house begins to take shape as lumber and steel are used to create the inner structure. Walls, windows, and doors define the internal structure. Walls and doors create boundaries and privacy. They serve to keep people out and to keep you in. Windows are flexible boundaries; they can be opened to let in fresh air and to invite connection with the outside world.

How many walls and doors do you want? Would you prefer an open floor plan? A split-level with staircases that lead to other floors? How accessible are you willing to be?

_____

_____

_____

INSTALLATION OF PLUMBING

Plumbing represents movement of materials within the system of a house, the "veins "that transport material in and out of the house. It maintains sanitary conditions, provides essential nourishment, heating and cooling. It maintains the flow. When a blockage occurs, the system backs up and restricts healthy flow and can create unsanitary conditions.

List potential issues that may cause blockages in the system.

_____

_____

_____

ELECTRICAL (ENERGY FLOW)

The electrical system represents the source of internal energy. Energy in the brain is the result of synapses firing. They are involved in formulating thoughts and memories, positive or negative. Negative thoughts fuel negative feelings which blocks the flow of positive energy. Faulty wiring causes fires.

List negative thoughts and feelings that may continue to block your flow of energy.

_____

_____

_____

MONITORING TEMPERATURE

The HVAC system regulates the temperature in your home. List thoughts, memories, situations that raise or lower your temperature (anger, worry, depression).

INSULATION

Insulation helps to maintain even temperature in the home, protects the home from moisture damage, and from mold growth. It helps to reduce the amount of energy (fossil fuel, natural gas, etc.) needed to maintain temperature.

Reflect on the purpose of insulation. What comes to mind? What type of insulation is best for you? Fiberglass? Cellulose? Cotton? Straw? Plastics? What type of insulation is unacceptable? Why?

CURING AND GRINDING DOWN, CREATING BOUNDARIES

Drywall creates walls and ceilings and helps with fire resistance. It can also be used in pieces to repair a hole in a wall. After it is installed, drywall requires slow and steady preparation before it is ready for painting and hanging wall art. It needs to be carefully spackled, primed, and sanded. It takes patience, time and concentration. Add a layer of spackle and wait for it to dry. Sand the spackle and add another layer. Sand again and add a layer of spackle until the drywall is smooth.

Preparation of drywall is a thoughtful process of shaping rough, raw material into a strong surface that provides safety, security and beauty. Cracks are filled and rough edges are smoothed.

Are there any painful thoughts and feelings that need to be ground down? Turn inward and check in—are there dark emotions such as shame hidden in the drywall that can cause cracks? List them now.

_____

_____

_____

EXTERIOR FINISHES

Exterior finishes refers to the external, the cosmetic, that which can be seen on the outside. Sprinklers, drainage systems, gutters, the driveway, patio, pool. The esthetics; the outer beauty; what you show the world. Reflect on the following:

How do you want to be seen? Do you want a long driveway, hidden from the street? Do you want your driveway to be gated? Will you plant flowers and grass? Cactus? Ground covering? What does a pool represent for you? Make a list of what you *don't* want and why.

FIXTURES AND FLOORING

Fixtures include lighting, ceiling fans, smoke detectors, garage doors, blinds, curtains, shutters hardware. Flooring includes, wood, carpet, tile, linoleum, bamboo, vinyl, laminate.

List the fixtures you no longer need. What fixtures have you always wanted? Do you want blackout curtains? No curtains? Why? What do blinds represent to you?

What does carpeting bring to mind? Would you prefer plush shag carpeting that covers your toes? The cool sensation of tile under your feet?

INSPECTION AND WALKTHROUGH

Do a careful inspection of your heroes' house. Are there any cracks, holes, missing tiles, radon or other toxins? Do you have everything you want in your home? Anything you want to remove? Is everything in working order?

FINAL RELEASE CEREMONY

Release any thoughts, feelings, fears, and beliefs that emerged during this exercise.

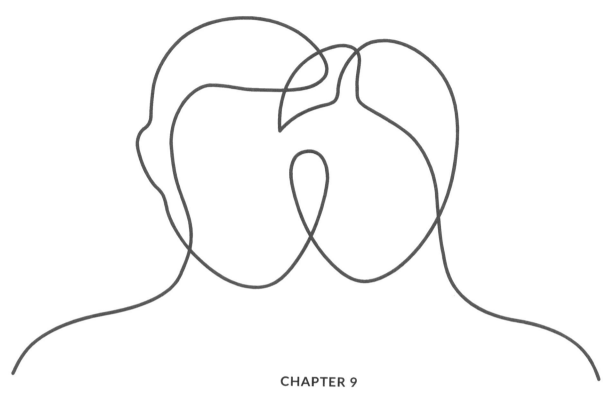

CHAPTER 9

RESTORATION AND RECLAIMING SELF

"Everything can be taken from a man but one thing: the last of the human freedoms—to choose one's attitude in any given set of circumstances, to choose one's own way."

~ Victor Frankl, *Man's Search for Meaning*

Truths have been faced. Battles were fought, trials, battles and challenges overcome. You are ready to move forward.

The restoration phase is all about finding meaning in life again. This doesn't mean you won't still have feelings of sadness or longing, but you will also have moments of happiness again. There are two tasks in this last phase of your journey: (1) To reclaim your life *with a new story which includes the bruises and scars bound together with gold, a Kintsugi story*; and (2) To restore you to wholeness. Your heroes' journey elevated your suffering to a sacred place. Before putting it all back together, you must find the meaning in your journey.

MAKING MEANING OUT OF SUFFERING

In his book *Man's Search for Meaning* (1945), Viktor Frankl, a holocaust survivor, said that even if you suffer, if you have purpose you will find strength. He said that there is no hope to remain alive if we perceive our suffering as useless. Finding purpose transforms suffering into a challenge. Dr. Frankl believed that in the worst of circumstances we have two choices: (1) To assume that we cannot change what happens to us, leaving our only choice to be a prisoner of our circumstance, or (2) To accept that we cannot change what happened to us but that we can change our attitude toward it. A stronger, resilient and positive attitude allows us to realize our lives' meaning. For Dr. Frankl, to realize his purpose he had to take responsibility for his life to be of help to others. He stated that by having a clear purpose, or "why" we are alive allows us to face the "how" questions of life.

 EXERCISE: Contemplate

What do you believe to be the reason this category 6 hurricane blew apart your safe home and wreaked havoc in your life? Why now? Had you been yearning for fulfillment and intimacy from your betrayer, trying to build a connection? Were you wishing for something different? What blessing did this hurricane bring to you? What did you need to learn?

What wisdom did you acquire that will aid in the healing of others? What insight, what "potion" do you have that, when you use it, will fortify you and continue to provide the strength needed to live your heroes' life with a higher purpose?

What is your life's purpose? What is your mission in this lifetime?

ABOUT THOSE PUZZLE PIECES...

Reflect back to those painful months after discovery. The confusion, anxiety, fear, and that surreal sense that "this can't be happening." Courageously, you accepted the call to action, and off you went, to fight two-headed dragons, villains, and meet allies along the way. You spent time looking into the "mirror of reality" and met your dark side; your most vulnerable and wounded parts. You released it all; thoughts, attitudes, feelings, and behaviors that needed to be understood, acknowledged, witnessed, forgiven, and ceremoniously let go to make way for a new path.

You began building your heroes' house when you stepped into your heroes' journey. You are ready to return back to your world. Your world probably hasn't changed that much, although, considering that your relationship house was bombed, it is probably worse.

ONE OF MY FAVORITE ANALOGIES

You are learning to make meaning out of your suffering and in so doing you are in a state of transformation, metamorphosis. When you began your journey, you were a cucumber. With each exercise you traveled deeper into your suffering and learned to tolerate and even to accept the bitterness, the sour and, even at times, sweetness. You broke, put yourself back together, and broke again. (You will probably break again but this time you will have an emergency trauma toolkit!). The change is cellular. You are now a pickle and there's no going back to being a cucumber!

A truth that you will continue to face is that you may not know everything. Your betrayer may have been completely honest and transparent; or he may be withholding information, keeping secrets. At this point, you realize that another piece of information no longer has as much value, one way or the other, because in your wise self you know that you are strong and loved no matter what—even in the eye of the storm. You know yourself. Your intuition is connected and you are now able to listen to *your* wisdom to guide important decisions about *your* life. Your wellness is not defined by your betrayer's behavior because you will feel the change in your betrayer.

There may be omissions, or floating "puzzle pieces." How will your "*I need to know everything*" parts live peacefully if all of the puzzle pieces are not in place? Remember, you are the captain of your ship.

 EXERCISE: Completing the Puzzle

You will need a large sheet of paper, colored markers and pencils, and scissors. Ask a question to your inner world, to your parts: How many puzzle pieces are missing? Draw them now. Draw the puzzle piece shapes, including the interlocking tabs and slots.

What do these puzzle pieces represent?

- Endless obsession and suffering?

- Chronic suspicion and mistrust?

- Acceptance of what is?

- Releasing attachment to the control that puzzle piece has over you?

- Freedom?

It is time to choose a side. Write or draw on each puzzle piece what it symbolizes. The puzzle is complete. The "*I need to know everything*" part can relax.

TAKING BACK YOUR POWER

Empowerment begins with reevaluating the situation with an expanded perspective. We begin by remembering that there are at least three truths in every story:

1. Your experience of the situation, or your truth;

2. The other person's experience of the story, or their truth;

3. And the story as told by an observer.

Taking back your power requires that you look at all sides of the issue. As difficult as it is to imagine that you may have a "side," the painful truth is that we all do.

THIS EXERCISE IN NO WAY IMPLIES THAT YOU HAVE
RESPONSIBILITY FOR YOUR BELOVED TO BETRAY YOU.

 EXERCISE: The Final Version of Your Story

Your story is now informed by the battles you fought and the insights you gained along the way. This is the *real* story, warts and all. Use the writing prompts to help you to retell the story of your life.

*   Describe the challenges you have overcome and the strengths that it took to do so.

- Describe your life today and who you are now.

- How do you differ from your past self?

- What are your challenges now?

- What are your strengths today?

- Describe your future. How will your life be different than it is today?

- How will you be different than you are today?

- What do you need to do to achieve the dreams of your future?

- What is your purpose today?

When you are finished writing your story, close the workbook, step outside and take in your world with all of your senses; sound, smell, taste, sight, feeling, and intuition. When you are ready, read your story aloud. Notice how that was with all of your senses. When the time is right, share your story with your betrayer. If you are in a betrayal trauma support group, read your story to the members.

READ YOUR STORY UNTIL **IT BECOMES YOUR STORY.**

EXERCISE: Restoration of Self

It is time to welcome all parts of you and celebrate you!

All of your work comes together now as you welcome all parts of you to make themselves known and heard. All parts of you have gifts to share. This final exercise is sacred. Accepting and loving all parts of yourself is the path to joy and peace.

Integration: The Parts Party Process

1. With your eyes closed, imagine being in a place in nature where you feel very comfortable. And, while exploring this place in nature, notice a rectangular table with six chairs around it.

2. Ask your unconscious mind for two parts of yourself which you really enjoy. And when they arrive, welcome them, as they take their seats at the table. Introduce them to each other.

3. Ask your unconscious mind for two parts of yourself which you find useful and practical in some way. And when they arrive, welcome them, as they take their seats at the table, then introduce everyone there.

4. Ask your unconscious mind for two parts of yourself which you particularly dislike. And when they arrive, welcome them, as they take their seats at the table, then introduce every one there.

5. Say to all the parts at the table, "Please tell me who here feels the most misunderstood?" Notice which one responds. And now ask the one who feels most misunderstood, "What is your positive purpose, the gift you bring to

me?" Listen to the answer. And notice that the others understand and appreciate the importance of this part's gift.

6. Say to the remaining five parts, "Who among you feels the most misunderstood?" And ask the one who responds, "What is your positive purpose, the gift you bring to me?" Listen to the answer. And notice that the others understand and appreciate the importance of this part's gift.

7. Say to the remaining four parts, "Who among you feels the most misunderstood?" And ask the one who responds, "What is your positive purpose, the gift you bring to me?" Listen to the answer. And notice that the others understand and appreciate the importance of this part's gift.

8. Say to the remaining three parts, "Who among you feels the most misunderstood?" And ask the one who responds, "What is your positive purpose, the gift you bring to me?" Listen to the answer. And notice that the others understand and appreciate the importance of this part's gift.

9. Say to the remaining parts, "I've welcomed the other parts to this table; I'd like to welcome you, as well. Please tell me, one at a time, the gift you bring to me." Listen to their answers. And notice that the others understand and appreciate the importance of the gifts these parts bring.

10. Watch as the six parts create a circle of gifts by holding hands with each other. And, as the table fades away, stand in the middle of the circle of gifts, and allow this inner-team to merge in the center of your heart, breathing it into your lungs, your bones and blood stream.

11. And now touch the base of your throat to anchor this new integration. And you can let the feeling you have now take you all the way into your past, to just before you were born. Be in your mother's womb feeling this way. And as both sperm and egg, allow yourself to continue going back into all the branches of your family history. And now, with this integrated feeling deeply within your history, your body and your cellular structure, gently bring it forward through all the branches of your family and years of your life to this present moment. Now, watch it continue to gently unfold into your future.

12. As you let go of the throat–anchor, notice what your life will feel like from now on with this integration totally within you.

CHAPTER 10

IS RECONCILIATION POSSIBLE?

Yes, reconciliation is possible. When both people are in individual therapy with a Certified Sex Addiction Therapist or betrayed partner specialist, working independently, and also working together as a couple, there is a very strong chance they can make the marriage work once again. Ultimately, the health of the relationship is dependent on the betrayer getting the right kind of help, and not based on the type of "acting out" behavior.

But, when the person struggling with addiction is the only one working on recovery and the partner has the attitude that "this is your problem, not mine," the prognosis is much lower. Remember, the work is deep—the betrayer and the betrayed are on their own heroes' journey. If either partner doesn't accept their call to action, they may feel better immediately, but it is a band–aid. A scab will form but the infection will continue to live deep down below the surface, lying in wait for the next storm. DO YOUR WORK NOW so you can live joyfully later.

The information and exercises ahead are intended to give you a wider, expanded sense of the state of your relationship today so that you both know where to go from here. We believe couples therapy is an essential part of building your relationship house.

TRUST BUILDING: THE FIRST STEP OF RECONCILIATION

Review the trust building questions with your partner:

- What I want to know from you is whether I can count on you, depend on you?

- Will you be there for me?

- Will you respond to me when I call?

- Do I matter to you?

- Am I the priority in your life?

- Am I valued and accepted by you?

- Now that you know my needs, what do you need from me?

DO WE SHARE THE SAME BASIC GOALS?

Successful relationships are ones in which partners share core values and goals. At the same time, each partner is an individual within the relationship with their own interests, values, and goals. In relationships there exists an "I," a "*thou*," and a "*we*." Each person is responsible for 100% of their 50% of the relationship. In other words, each person gives 100% to the relationship. One person cannot hold a relationship together—although betrayed partners often over-function by *necessity*.

In her book *Hold Me Tight*, Sue Johnson states that the cornerstone of a relationship is: you are my beloved; wherever in the world I am, you are my home; you have my back.

 EXERCISE: Relationship Values

Below is a list of values, qualities and needs and expectations in relationships. Circle the five that are most important for you today. Put a check mark next to those that need attention. Underline those that are of concern and address them soon.

Continued growth work	Managing own emotions
Shared agreement on finances	Sexual (self & partner) are our values aligned?
Beliefs toward self and other	Privacy
Sympathy	Interest/curiosity
Needs are valued and met	Joy/support for growth
Honesty	Humor
Acceptance	Hellos and good-byes
Protection	Control
Work through conflict	Fidelity
Individual interests/hobbies	Physical
Spiritual	Admiration
Safety	Relational
Intellectual	Community

Conflict resolution	Having difficult conversations
Shared rituals	Supporting one another's dreams
Affection	Aspirations
Tolerance	Philanthropy

Values we share include:

_____

_____

As we consider reconciliation, I need:

_____

_____

One of my concerns about my partner moving forward is:

_____

_____

For me, reconciliation looks like:

_____

_____

In order to continue in the reconciliation process, I need:

_____

_____

THE IMPORTANCE OF CONNECTION IN HEALING BETRAYAL TRAUMA

"I have found solace in talking to a trusted friend or family member. I suggest you join a betrayed partners group and find someone you can confide in who won't judge you or your spouse. A big portion of healing for me was being able to talk about what was going on in my life with others. If you have a faith, any faith or belief in a higher power, turn to that; study your religion, embrace prayer, and be open to whatever guidance you feel. No matter what happens in your relationship, know you are valued by a higher power and your happiness does matter."

HOW A PARTNER BEGAN HER PERSONAL JOURNEY TOWARD RECONCILIATION:

"Number one, for me, in that healing was to learn what healthy boundaries were and consult with a professional to set boundaries to protect myself emotionally and physically. I remember I set a boundary that my husband could only have $30 cash on him at a time. This was a big change since he often had hundreds of dollars on him. I told my therapist this boundary and she said, "Actually, you have the right to ask him to give up his debit card." I remember thinking, "Wow, I can ask that much?" I would have never set that boundary as strongly without her guidance and support. Number two, you cannot do this on your own. No matter what happens in your relationship, know you are valued by a higher power and your happiness does matter."

A sign in my office reads: $$\frac{\text{BEHAVIOR}}{\text{TIME}} = \textbf{TRUST}$$

Building trust requires that you are patient and self–restrained. Strategies in your trauma toolkit and emergency toolkit will help keep fear and anxiety in check. Trust is built on one right decision and one right behavior at a time. All of the ways betrayed partners use to reassure themselves that they are safe end up making them more anxious and, therefore, less safe. The most common ways include asking them if they are "okay" (which is "code" for are you sober), expecting them to tell you about what was discussed in 12-step meetings and therapy sessions, calling on a landline to be sure they are where they say they are, doing a "drive-by" to see if they are where they say they are, checking their cell phone without them knowing, reading their emails, confronting them about anything, expecting them to stop hanging out with friends and discontinue business trips among others.

Your betrayer cannot gain your trust unless you allow them to!

After disclosure, your best strategy is to do nothing and observe everything. In the context of your heroes' journey, consider this to be a trial to overcome. Your weapon for this battle is patience. Your tool is the following:

SIT ON YOUR HANDS, KEEP YOUR MOUTH CLOSED AND KEEP YOUR EYES OPEN

You have been working hard and have the calmness, composure, and self-awareness needed to use your observational skills, your gut, and intuition to assess whether your betrayer is trustworthy.

WHAT WILL I OBSERVE THAT WILL INDICATE MY BETRAYER IS BECOMING TRUSTWORTHY?

- They sought help with a CSAT and disclosed it.

- They are contrite.

- They are aware of mess-ups and own it.

- They made a choice to stay in the relationship to work on healing.

- They are working hard to stop staring/flirting behavior.

- They try to help when I am struggling, even if they doesn't get it right.

- They have compassion.

- They are completely accountable with where they are at any time.

- They call when they are going to be late.

- They don't criticize me or get defensive when I am struggling.

- They want to be better.

- They are dependable.

- They initiate the check-In with compassion.

- They admit slips with sexually compulsive behavior.

- They put your need for comfort and safety above their needs.

RELATIONSHIP TOOLKIT: COMMUNICATION

Clear communication is essential right now. Make a copy of the open-ended questions, the feelings list, and Five-Step Communication tool and put them on your refrigerator.

OPEN-ENDED QUESTIONS

Open-ended questions encourage conversation and help the speaker to feel heard and understood. Healthy couples work hard to avoid starting sentences with "You (always/never)" or "Why (do you/don't you ever)?" as these are criticisms disguised as questions. Begin sentences with:

- I'm curious about...

- Tell me more about...

- Help me understand...

- I'm confused about...

- How did...?

- What are the ways _____ is affecting your life?

- How did you feel about...?

- How important is _____ to you?

- How did you discover, learn about _____ ?

- How are you feeling about _____?

- What happened when _____ ?

- What is your fear about _____ ?

- What do you wish for?

- Will you explain more about _____ ?

- I wonder why_____?

- What do you worry would happen if_____ ?

- What will happen next?

- What do you need right now?

- What would the result be if_____?

- What do you believe?

- What options do you see right now?

- I'd like to hear more about...

<u>*FIVE-STEP COMMUNICATION TOOL*</u>

1. When I heard you say _____ *or*
   When I saw _____ *or*
   When I discovered _____ .

2. The story I make up about it is _____ *or*
   I'm assuming that _____ .

3. And, as a result, I am feeling _____.

4. And that reminds me of_____ my childhood, *or*
   And that reminds me of the time you _____.

5. I need clarification. Is my assumption correct?
   If not, what did you intend for me to know?
   With clarification, I feel _____ *and*
   I need _____ .

COUPLES CHECK-IN: BUILDING TRUST ON A CONSISTENT BASIS

<u>*GUIDELINES*</u>

- The betrayer (or person struggling with sex addiction) initiates check-in. The number of times per week is to be determined by partner/spouse.

- Limit time of check in. No more than ½ hour is suggested to minimize triggers for partner.

- All questions are acceptable to ask (maintain respect).

- It is often helpful for the partner to hold questions for check-in to insure that partner's emotional needs are met.

PURPOSE/RATIONALE

This check-in serves to:

- Increase relational trust.

- Demonstrate active recovery.

- Promote honesty and the spirit of transparency.

- Decrease partner anxiety, or "triggers."

- Promote adult/adult relating.

The betrayer (or person struggling with sex addiction) states question aloud and then answers the question.

1. How am I feeling physically, emotionally and spiritually?

2. How many "S: meetings have I attended since the last check-in? State the location of the meetings.

3. Report any acting-out behavior since the last check-in (do not include details that will create an image). Please report behavior only. Reporting thoughts is not suggested, as thoughts are commonly intrusive and unwelcome, and therefore, not considered "acting out". However, allowing the thought to develop into a fantasy is considered "acting out" which is to be reported.

4. Partner is invited to ask questions. If the conversation becomes contentious, it is best to discontinue.

5. Betrayer asks partner feeling-oriented questions about how they are coping with their trauma, or "trigger" feelings and reactions related to the check-in, seeking to offer a perspective of care (empathy) toward the partner.

6. Betrayer asks partner for feedback: Have you felt heard by me? Have you felt understood by me? Have I treated you with respect? Have I been adequately humble and deferring to your needs?

7. Betrayer offers a statement of gratitude to the partner.

8. Check-in ends with the serenity prayer (optional).

SERENITY PRAYER

GOD GRANT ME THE SERENITY

TO ACCEPT THE THINGS I CANNOT CHANGE

COURAGE TO CHANGE THE THINGS I CAN

AND THE WISDOM TO KNOW THE DIFFERENCE

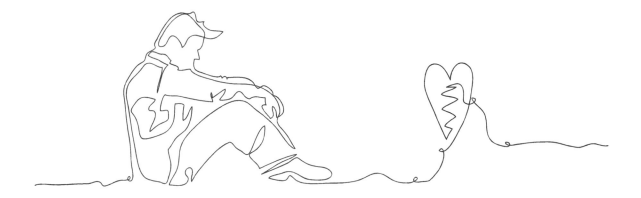

CHAPTER 11

WHAT PEOPLE IN RECOVERY FROM SEX ADDICTION WANT YOU TO KNOW

In the same way that many betrayed partners who have transformed their suffering into meaning are moved to aid in the healing of those that come after them, their betrayers find purpose in helping those that are surviving betrayal trauma. We asked clients currently in treatment if they were interested in contributing to betrayed partners' healing. They appreciated the opportunity to offer anything that would be of help. Those who contributed wish to offer a sincere prayer for your heart healing. They also want you to know that good help is available and it is not your job to take care of them and that, although they are lost and despairing, they can get all the help they need. And, beware, they are still lying and manipulating.

BETRAYER IN RECOVERY FROM SEX ADDICTION

Recovery is a long process, and just like you feel you need your betraying partner to be patient with you, I need a lot of time to heal. I understand that your world has just crashed down around you, and, not only am I the cause of it, I am completely incapable of empathizing or helping you in a meaningful way.

I want you to know, I didn't just wake up one morning and make the conscious decision to be addicted to sex, porn, sexting, or chat rooms. I never intended to be unfaithful since the day we met. My intentions were never to hurt you. When I think about it, there was always a feeling that I had a hole in my soul and I never knew how to fill it up properly. A gnawing, anxious feeling that something was missing, but I wasn't sure where it was so I could grab it and fill up the wound. Instead, I always felt emotionally stunted in my growth as a human being. Always searching for someone, anyone, to validate my worthiness as a necessary part of society.

AN EXAMPLE OF WHAT RUNS THROUGH MY MIND

It seems I've spent my entire life seeking to medicate a gnawing feeling of inadequacy. Anger, resentment, frustration, fear, sadness, and loneliness have made my life a living hell. Internally I ask the negative voice in my head, "Why do you continually threaten my sanity?" Isn't it enough that for the past dozen years you have destroyed my ambition? You've convinced me to turn aside my good qualities and strengths and focus instead on destructive distractions that will eventually kill me spiritually and physically. Why must you cover me in your blanket of shame and guilt, further alienating me from my spirit and from the people I love?"

The loud shame messages of my past continue to haunt me. "I'm not good enough, smart enough, creative enough, handsome enough." Therefore, I must be a failure and resign myself that this is all I'm entitled to. I sometimes feel like crying in mourning for having to live believing in these shame messages rather than appreciating and being grateful for you and the love we once shared. Voices in my head convince me that you do not give me enough attention and sex and that it's because I am unloveable.

I end up feeling entitled to screw up and act out. Anxiety racks my body with shock waves because the pull of addiction is always in the driver's seat.

I'VE BETRAYED THE LOVE OF MY LIFE

In my usual victim role, dug up from my past, I feel powerless, unworthy, alone and afraid, loved yet lonely. The payoff for me is to get sympathy for what I've been through and I feel entitled to escape into a fantasy world or eat my way out of a potato chip bag. All I really want is unconditional love. Early on in our relationship I was the rescuer; powerful, charitable, helpful, and popular. My payoff was to be the hero, to feel important and worthy of someone else's love. I wanted to be able to give love without holding resentment for helping someone. This was difficult because, in my life, I believed that helping and doing for others always came with strings attached. I created walls between me and those I loved.

The events and crisis that brought me to recovery were incredibly painful. My whole life I've been searching for meaning outside myself. I'm not comfortable in my own skin, instead, alone and afraid to be myself. I've spent my life matching my insides to other people's outsides and comparing. This produces profound shame and brings up unconscious feelings of not being good enough. It's as if I'm being told, "Don't talk because you'll say something stupid." "Let everyone else take care of you, don't get involved, make waves, or stand up for yourself." This makes me feel worse and I sink into depression—alone, afraid, and with no power, energy, or will to go on living.

CHAPTER 11: WHAT PEOPLE IN RECOVERY FROM SEX ADDICTION WANT YOU TO KNOW

I HAVE NO IDEA WHO I AM:

Instead of trying to help you, I push you away again and again. Discovery caused me to face how empty I am inside and how cunningly deceptive I can be. In the end, it leads to loneliness. I sit alone and don't talk to anyone in my own house. I alienate myself from family and friends who simply try to get close. I have never believed that anyone really loved me, including you. When you reach out, I shut down. I can't handle being close.

Acting out in addiction, in some weird way, protects me from emotional pain. At the beginning, it was the only way I knew to rid myself of pressure about what everyone else expected of me. The addiction protects me from feeling inept. I can't be truthful about what I want or need. I expect things to be a certain way and when they don't turn out as I expect, I protect myself. The only way I know how is to shut down, turn to rage, turn it around to make you believe it's really your fault, and then use sex to feel better.

I AM IMMATURE. I LOOK LIKE AN ADULT, BUT I AM REALLY A CHILD INSIDE.

I didn't know myself and waited for others to tell me what I should be doing and how to get there. I got depressed when I didn't get attention. I wanted whatever I wanted and did not even consider you. It is pathetic to admit, but it is true. The reason I was shocked when you confronted me is because I truly believed that I was entitled to do whatever I wanted to. And although I know that there is good in my life, I can't see it.

I want you to know that none of this is an excuse for my actions which hurt you deeply, making you feel unworthy, alone and afraid to trust me. Just know that the above thoughts and feelings are real; and today, after working on recovery, you can rest assured that the person you fell in love with years ago, is still in there, somewhere, ready to be vulnerable enough to let you experience *"in to me you see,"* healthy intimacy, possibly for the first time.

THE THINGS THAT MIGHT BE HELPFUL TO A PARTNER

- Overall message: Be as patient as you can, and then be patient a little more. Give it time. Recovery is a (long) process.

- Things the addicts say now should be taken with an understanding of this;. your world has just crashed down around you, and the same is true for the addicts. Everything they have known is uncertain. They are afraid of everything—what people will think, losing their families, losing their jobs, losing their friends, what their kids will think of them now and in 5 years and in 25 years. So, with all this uncertainty and change, what they say is not the "final answer." Don't hold them accountable for that forever. For example, they might say that they think their partners have some fault in this (because people tell them it's never just one person...). And in 6 months, they might not believe that at all. Remembering that this was said and assuming that it is still what the addicts think is likely an inaccurate assumption. Give them room to figure things out about themselves and their lives to date. The addicts' view on this will change for the next several years. What is said now is often said in panic and with very little information. Their amygdala is messed up!

- The addicts don't have answers for all your questions right away. (See above— world crashing in around them causes massive confusion—answer that will likely change one or more times in the next few years.) Demanding answers on the spot may result in the addicts giving the answers they think you want— because they can't think clearly enough to reason it out and giving the answers they think you want may be all they've ever known. Also, they don't really have many answers—after all, they are about to undergo the biggest change in their lives to date—rediscovering who they are, what their values are; understanding how pervasive the addiction was in their lives (i.e., not just "acting out" behaviors but all interactions); challenging their own spirituality, etc. Try to let them have time and space to do so. Ask the critical and urgent things: Do they want to be in the marriage? Are they committed to getting better? (Do they show that?) Is living with what has happened something you can do? What do you need to feel safe in the relationship while the recovery process for both of you unfolds? You have time for all the rest of the questions.

- Knowing all the details of the addictive behaviors, the acting out, may or may not be beneficial. Once you've heard it, you can't un-hear it. For example, knowing places where the addict acted out that you might drive by every day can re-traumatize you daily. Consider what will work best for you and ask the addict to respect that.

I'M SICKER THAN YOU REALIZE

The truth is that I can't be honest right now. I will try my hardest to answer your questions, but my answers will likely be dishonest; I have been lying to myself for so long that I don't know how to be honest. I don't want you to think I'm just "checking the boxes." I have to learn to be vulnerable, and right now, that is unfamiliar territory to me.

I will apologize constantly and expect that you will get over everything. In the first six months, I will believe that I have changed. I will tell you that I am not *that* person anymore. I will promise that it will never happen again, and I will be convincing. I will be tearful and look defeated—but it's mostly because I don't want to be alone. Because I am seeing a CSAT, going to three meetings a week, in a therapy group that holds me accountable for my behavior, have a sponsor, talk to other members of my group, and read whatever my therapist suggests, I will learn to have empathy for you and think more about you than I do about myself. That won't happen for another year. In the meantime, please take care of yourself and get the help you need.

VOICES FROM THOSE IN RECOVERY

"He's lying. He's lying. He's lying."

~ John, *a man in recovery from sex addiction*

"Although it is very difficult, if the partner is able to take childhood trauma into consideration and they are able to have even a little bit of empathy for the person who was caught, it will help the partner in their healing."

~ Mike, *in recovery from childhood neglect and sex addiction*

"When he tells you that he loves you, he means it. The problem has always been that he has never known what it means to love. He thought that being the breadwinner was how men showed their love. When you asked how he could cheat on you if he really loved you, the truth is that he never knew what it meant to love or feel love. He has become an expert at looking like he does, though."

~ Jim

"Lying is automatic: it has become the default. I lie about everything—it doesn't matter what the issue is or whether it even matters."

"I've been lying since I was seven years old, and my stepfather beat me if I got into trouble."

"I need you to know that what you are expecting is impossible now. Your sex-addicted partner can't explain why acting out with other people or on the computer was acceptable. He can't tell you why he did it. He can't tell you why he never thought of you."

"Here is what is true—he has no idea. If he knew why, he would have stopped or got help. There is no logic or reason with this behavior."

"You are desperate to understand and make sense of his secret life, I know. He has no answer that will give you any comfort or peace."

"I want you to know that I was as shocked as you were on D-Day. I was living in a fantasy world where none of my acting out was wrong or bad. I spent so many years in that fantasy that, at some point, it was real to me."

"I have no idea who I am or if there is anything inside that resembles a person. Inside is empty. The person you have been married to has been covered up by the person you see. I learned how to be who you needed me to be in order to make it through the day. It is painful, but it is the truth."

"My best advice is this: don't ask questions like 'did you ever love me?' We have a distorted idea of what love is. To us, love is putting a roof over our heads. Love is buying gifts. We don't feel anything inside—other than anger."

"You had no idea what was going on because I never told you anything. I didn't talk to you about work stress, stress at home—nothing. I learned that it is better to deal with things alone."

CHAPTER 12

FOR THE BETRAYER

HELPFUL TIPS FROM RECOVERING ADDICTS

FROM JOHN, A RECOVERING ADDICT

- Overall message: Try like hell to understand what your partner is going through. Keep your mouth shut and listen. Answer direct questions directly and with honesty.

- Shut up! First of all, you think you know something about why you did what you did—but you have a lot to learn. Second, you think that your addiction was the affair or strip clubs, or internet pornography but—it was so much more than that. It permeated all of your life, and you won't be able to see how fully it did so for a long time; maybe years. Your understanding of your addiction and of yourself will grow over time. Try not to say anything as definitive.

- Accept responsibility but don't try to explain. Explaining things right now just sounds like justification.

- Never avoid a conversation because you don't want to have it. But do have boundaries around when/where (i.e., not after 10 pm or not while at work, or not with others present).

- Try to say things like:

  - *"I hear you and understand what you are saying, and I know what I've done is so painful."*

  - *"Yes, I did that. It was terrible, and I know it hurt you at your core."*

  - *"I want to carefully consider what you are saying and asking, and I can't do that right now in front of you because there is too much on the line here and I'm anxious and worried I am not able to think as clearly as I'd like. I've hurt you too much already and want to make sure I'm clear. Can I have some time to work through this by myself? (Then go call a friend!)"*

- When you answer your partner's questions, do so with full honesty. Do not hold something back because you think it will further hurt your case. When your partner finds out things in dribs and drabs, it re-traumatizes them with every new piece of information. Trying to hide something now makes it worse later. If you think it is something that they will wish they didn't hear, you can hold off on that but need to immediately talk to a friend or sponsor or therapist to discuss it. And if you decide to tell them, do so as soon as possible and tell them truthfully why you didn't do so in the moment and what you did to come to the decision to tell them. (Show your process!)

"Just own it. Own it all."

~ Mike, *in recovery from sex addiction*

"Looking back, I feel as though I made most of the mistakes possible that a newly discovered person could. The one big thing my wife and I did correctly I feel was not making a decision on the relationship for 6 months. That gave us some time, allowed for us to start making sense of things, and become educated on sex addiction. When we hit our 6 month mark, we continued with another six months.

"Some advice for the first 6 months is get help! For both the addict and partner, separate help, and experienced sex addiction help. I started by seeing a drug and alcohol addiction counselor, their advice and premise was good for those substances, but not for sexuality. "Just don't do it" and "look away and distract your thoughts" and other complete abstinence plans are confusing and complicated for sex addiction. This is where a therapist with CSAT training is valuable and needed. Disclosure will likely come up and I'd advise it in most cases, and soon. Your partner will want answers and information. In my experience, I wish it had been sooner, a staggered disclosure was a nightmare for her, we didn't know what to do or how to do it, and the result was us fumbling through the first stages of discovery.

"I'd recommend a 12-step program also. There are a few for sex-addicted individuals, some also focus on the other components that are often part of the road leading to someone reading about this topic. Relationships, family, abuse, neglect, suppression, confusion, feelings, identity, and more are discussed in some 12-step groups and can be a great supplement to individual therapy. Twelve step provides a safe place with people that understand, can provide wisdom and support, and the start to forming a healthy support network. For me, it was life-saving to know I wasn't alone, and that there are many possible outcomes, I once again had control over who I wanted to be."

~ Pete, also in recovery from sex addiction

WHAT YOU CAN EXPECT IN SEX ADDICTION TREATMENT

Recovery is a progressive revealing of truths; and, like learning a new language, it takes fortitude, commitment, and patience. Recovery is hard work. Expect it to be the most challenging work of your life. You will learn how to identify feelings and how to manage them. You will learn how to break harmful patterns of thinking and feeling that ultimately lead to acting out.

Negative and self-destructive thinking will be replaced with self-respect. Dopamine, which excites the brain and drives lustful sexual thoughts and behavior, will shift to a lust for life. Cravings and unwelcome thoughts will subside over time as you live in integrity with your values.

THE FIRST YEAR

In the first two years of recovery, many people who seek help for compulsive sexual behavior have a similar experience. The first three months are easy. You were caught, and it was horrific. You're in shock, but you made it through alive. Therapy helps you to stay sober and to tolerate feeling your feelings while offering compassion to your devastated partner. Twelve-step meetings are eye-opening. Meeting other people who have the same compulsion is liberating. Their stories will inspire you to dive in and become a part of the recovering community. You will have support, people to call when you are struggling. You will feel shaky but hopeful.

The second three months begin to get tough. The "luster" and novelty will wear off as you face the extent of your behaviors. Guilt and shame set in, and your recovering community becomes your lifeline. Use all of your tools to stay sober. If you remain sober for the first three months, you will build the skills to manage the guilt and shame you will face in the second three months. The cravings should decrease in frequency and intensity. If you stay sober no matter what, your brain will start rewiring.

The second six months are difficult for a different reason. You will begin to yearn for the acting-out behavior. It is not easy living in the real world and, for the first time, *feeling* the stress. It was the only source you could turn to for relief from the hurt, anger, resentment and other intense emotions. There are several truths; your preferred type of acting out caused a catastrophic injury to your beloved, and it was your most cherished source of comfort. It never rejected you and never let you down. To get well, you must acknowledge this truth and grieve this loss. At the same time, you will face the pain you have caused and work hard to make right what you made wrong, to make reparations. You will use your coping skills to be comforting and accessible. You will offer empathy and compassion toward your hurting partner to heal your relationship.

RECOVERY FROM SEX ADDICTION/COMPULSIVE SEXUAL BEHAVIOR

There are three elements of recovery; physical, emotional, and spiritual. Physical recovery refers to all of your secretive behaviors. Make a list of all of the behaviors that are shameful, secretive, and compulsive. Become ready to stop acting out and to start getting honest with yourself.

Emotional sobriety is emotional balance. It is the ability to feel inner peace. Intense emotions become manageable. You will develop the ability to live in the present moment without the need or desire to self-medicate.

Spiritual recovery refers to being in connection to a higher power and to fellow man; to be a part of society. For those who are tempted to repel getting help because of the higher power element; stop and check yourself. What is more important—your feelings and false pride or owning up to the harm your choices caused and that you could not stop on your own?

DO NOT USE "FEELINGS" ABOUT A HIGHER POWER TO AVOID RECOVERY.

IF YOUR BELIEFS, FEELINGS, DISCOMFORT, AND PRIDE ARE MORE IMPORTANT
THAN YOUR BELOVED, TELL YOUR PARTNER NOW.
DON'T CAUSE THEM ANY MORE PAIN.

If you want to save your relationship, aid in the healing of your partner, and rescue yourself, **don't think further about a higher power**. Right now, in the middle of the crisis, follow the recommendations of the experts (CSAT and partner specialist therapists). You can revisit the issue with your therapist. Remember that *your best thinking got you here*. It may take about a month for you to feel more clear-headed. It takes on average ninety days for the dopamine in the brain to return to normal; in other words, it takes about ninety days to detox. Expect to fantasize, obsess, have urges, flashbacks and feel foggy-headed.

Recovery encompasses much more than the compulsive sexual behavior. It is an illness of self; a fracturing of the insides; the very core self is unreachable. Getting sober is just the beginning of the recovery process. The real work begins when you begin your inner hero's journey and face all of your "two-headed dragons" and reclaim your authentic self.

There are two important goals of recovery. The first is to get sober and stay sober *no matter what*. Slips happen *and* the goal is sobriety. The second goal of recovery is to mend relationships—if it's not too late. Building trust involves embracing and expressing responsibility for the harm you caused and doing whatever it takes to allow your partner to feel safe. It takes an average of 18 months for your betrayed partner's post-traumatic symptoms to decrease. **Your job is to do your work**. Begin working with a Certified Sex Addiction Therapist (www.iitap.com), attend individual and group therapy, attend 12-step meetings, complete readings and workbooks assigned by your therapist, seek a sponsor (a sober person who has experienced what you are going through), and become a part of the recovering community. *Recovery is not a hobby that you do when you have time and are in the mood.* Recovery is the work of your life and will probably be the most difficult undertaking of your life. If you do what is recommended, you will live a life of freedom, connection, and joy!

IS GROUP THERAPY NECESSARY?

Yes. Sex addiction thrives in secrecy and isolation. Most people with sex addiction are afraid of intimacy and feel awkward and anxious in social situations. Many admit they have never had close friends and don't believe they can trust anybody. They don't trust their partner or themselves. As Dr. Patrick Carnes says in Facing the Shadow, "It [acting out] is an alternative to letting oneself feel hurt, betrayal, worry and—most painful of all—loneliness." Group therapy helps heal the deep sense of emptiness and loneliness. It offers you the opportunity to share your shame with people who understand and support you without judgment. Without it, you remain alone and isolated in shame and guilt with no way out but to resort to the old, reliable, and destructive source of comfort. Group members practice honesty, vulnerability, and how to handle difficult discussions. Most importantly, the group serves as a bridge to be vulnerable with your partner.

FACING YOUR PAST

Revisiting your past is a necessary step in understanding how you ended up where you are today. In your recovery journey, you will learn about all of the conditions that led to your compulsive behavior. You will understand that negative beliefs about yourself resulting from childhood abuse and neglect, such as "*I'm not loveable,*" "*I'll never amount to anything,*" "*I shouldn't have done that,*" etc., are the driving force behind infidelity. Treatment with a CSAT will help you heal the childhood wounds that keep the negative beliefs alive.

It's essential to make this connection for yourself with your therapist's help, because knowledge of where addiction comes from is essential for your healing.

A GREAT TIP FROM A BETRAYED PARTNER TO THE BETRAYER

When your partner is feeling discouraged and is not expressing it to you, reach out to acknowledge her pain. It is a perfect moment to say, "I want you to know how grateful I am that you are allowing me to stay with you for today. I broke your heart. I intend to support you in any way that feels safe to you."

These are beautifully comforting, empathetic words, particularly when delivered at such a perfect moment. You can memorize the quote, modify it, or use your own words, whatever is most comfortable for you. The key is to include, in no particular order, the following:

1.   A statement of gratitude.

2.   An acknowledgment of your partner's pain.

3.   A positive intention.

Unfaithful spouses I've counseled often report that this most welcome surprise is the best thing they did to lift their partner's spirits—as well as their own.

COMMUNICATION PROMPTS

Miscommunication between couples in recovery is the main cause of problems. Those who grow up in homes in which family members are disengaged or enmeshed don't learn healthy communication skills. In recovery, gaining effective and compassionate skills facilitates the healing of relationship wounds.

Relationships recovering from betrayal and broken trust require particular care. The early stages of rebuilding trust require a special and strong effort to listen to, validate, and demonstrate keen understanding of the partner's pain.

ASK QUESTIONS

- Are there any questions you have for me?

- Have I listened to you today?

- Have I hurt you today?

- Have I been attentive, respectful, forthcoming, understanding, loving?

- Is there anything you need me to do today?

TAKE ACTIONS

- Express appreciation to your partner for their willingness to continue to remain married *today*.

- Express gratitude for something specific that your partner did today.

- Continue to do whatever you can to make amends—show your partner, don't tell them.

- Take full responsibility for the harm you caused to the family.

- Agree to a "No Secrets Contract." Commit to your partner that you will be truthful, forthcoming, and honest.

- Admit any acting out to your partner. Admit any lies to your partner.

- Ask your partner what is needed to feel safe today.

Recovery guided by a CSAT is not the same as a 12-step program. Therapeutic-driven recovery expects a level of honesty that differs from the 12-step program because therapy focuses on saving relationships, regaining relational integrity, and aiding in the healing of your partner's pain.

STOP APOLOGIZING

No "I'm sorries." Avoid making empty promises—**all promises are empty for partners**. Because of your history of dishonesty, your word means nothing today. Remember that only behavior over time equals trust.

SAVING THE MARRIAGE

Saving your marriage is your greatest challenge. Your betrayed partner has the right to express her anger, ask why this happened, and express the pain she feels due to being traumatized by your choices. Keep in mind that you have known all along that you were lying and cheating. Your partner had no idea. You chose to believe that your infidelity did not affect your relationship. In fact, it cracked the very foundation of the relationship. One betrayed spouse told her betrayer, *"When the marriage is important enough to you, and you really want it to work, you will do whatever it takes."*

ARE YOU READY TO DO WHATEVER IT TAKES?

Attending 12-step meetings, working with a sponsor, weekly therapy with a CSAT, working through workbooks assigned by your therapist, joining a therapist-led process group, talking with others in recovery outside of meetings for support are examples of doing "whatever it takes."

There is a vast difference between "checking the boxes" and fully engaging in healing from the inside out. Until the betrayer has made amends, remains contrite, and agrees to a therapist-led formal disclosure when recommended, the relationship cannot move forward. During formal disclosure, therapists collaborate to ensure safety, honesty, and, most important, so there will be no secrets, manipulation, avoidance, and any other means people use to avoid pain.

Additionally, healing family of origin trauma and examining attachment disorders are necessary for relationship healing, building intimacy, and to prevent relapse.

Betrayers are fortunate when their spouse or partner embraces healing. Your wounded partner will know that you are making progress when you are humble, caring, and compassionate toward her. You have to earn your injured partner's trust. Lack of empathy, humility, and compassion are red flags that a betrayer is not fully working his recovery program.

It is important to know that there will be a time when you will discuss your relationship needs; however, not until your betrayed partner feels safe and ready to work on reconciliation. Stating your needs now will be perceived as selfish and will reinforce hopelessness.

EXERCISE: Building Trust Back

What I plan to do to build trust back with my partner is:

Describe in detail how your actions have made your partner feel:

Make a Commitment:

You are reading this because, in some way, your partner got you here. Most people struggling with sex addiction don't usually admit to their secrets, lying, and infidelity until they are caught. If you are willing to do whatever it takes to get well, make that commitment now.

Resources for CSATs and partner specialists and 12-step meetings are in the appendix.

I commit to call a therapist _____

I commit to read _____

I commit to finding a 12-step meeting on zoom or in my area.

_____

WHAT TO DO WHEN CRAVINGS STRIKE?

Patrick Carnes, Ph.D. in A *Gentle Path through the Twelve Steps* (Hazelden, 1993, Center City, MN), offers action steps when your day is less than glorious. Again, it goes back to trusting yourself, your intuition, and asking for help. Just making it through another day is not enough to stay sober. You have to create boundaries for yourself to protect your sobriety and make recovery your priority. Learn to express your feelings healthily. Expressing feelings is the necessary pathway toward eventual healing. Admit your mistakes, set goals, and work toward them.

STRATEGIES TO MANAGE INTENSE EMOTIONS AND STAY SOBER

ACT DIALECTICALLY[11]

The word dialectic comes from the Greek word 'dialektikos,' which assumes that two seemingly opposite ideas can co-exist without diminishing the other. For example, it is possible to want to be sober and also want to abuse substances. It is possible to love someone and be mad at them at the same time. It is possible to be happy about one part of your life and sad about another.

For the trauma survivor or person struggling with addiction, this strategy helps with limited ways of thinking: black and white, good or bad, right or wrong, perfect or imperfect, while considering the grey area may be a more sensible choice to balance your life. We begin to accept that people may not believe what we believe, may not act like we think they should, and begin to practice a more middle path, balanced approach to life, feelings, and relationships.

When you experience a craving, you can use dialectic strategies to ride the wave of your feelings, like riding a wave in the ocean rather than acting on every impulse. Many people believe they need to act out when they are in a negative feeling state. Using dialectic strategies, you surf the emotion wave as it rises and increases in strength and then falls in a few moments.

People who struggle with addiction and trauma are overwhelmed by negative feelings and self-medicate with compulsive sexual behavior to escape the pain. Dialectical thinking makes room for the positive things in life to balance out the negative. Most of life happens in the grey areas. When you become triggered to act out sexually, the more you can think dialectically, the more you will surf your urges like a wave in the ocean. You will realize that the urge goes up and eventually comes down. Even in the moment of struggle, you will recognize that you have a choice. On the one hand, you want to act out sexually to feel better. On the other hand, you want to remain sober and not face additional consequences.

Examples of dialectic strategies include refusing to engage in all or nothing thinking, using metaphors or stories to see the situation differently, playing the "devil's advocate," and using wise-mind exercises.

PLAY THE TAPE OUT

Playing the tape out is a strategy to stop acting out in it's path. Playing the tape out involves imagining the rest of the story—not just the ecstasy of the high but also the guilt, shame, and despair that follows the euphoria. When you continue to play that scene to its end, the cravings subside because the fantasy of ecstasy also includes the horrible consequences that inevitably follow.

Slips and relapses don't happen out of the blue. Sometimes it can be a matter of hours, days, or months when we begin to feel disconnected from ourselves and reality, feeling restless, irritable, or discontent with life. One of the most effective techniques for maintaining sobriety amid emotional distress is the skill of playing the tape out. Think of the "tape" like a movie scene to reflect on what happens after the action. When you play the tape out in your mind, you discover that things won't turn out well. Play the tape out can be used in a positive sense also. With long-lasting sobriety, you can think about how good it felt to be sober and whether you want to go back to sleeping on the couch or risking getting caught.

 EXERCISE: Playing the Tape Out

Imagine that you are about to act out. This time, rather than acting on impulse, you are going to play the tape out. Like a movie scene, describe your story from the moment urges start until the acting out ends. Include your feelings throughout the scene. What are the consequences that happened the last time you acted out? Will a few moments of pleasure be worth the consequences?

_____

_____

_____

_____

_____

Now envision a positive scenario where you are living a sober life. Imagine what it will look like, hear the sounds of happiness from your partner and children, feel the good feelings of joy and happiness knowing you are doing the right thing.

STAY CALM

When a person is having a bad day or is under a lot of stress, it helps to have strategies to reduce inner stress so that they can remain calm, even in the eye of the storm. Examples of calming strategies include: visual—look around you and find circles; sound—listen to an oldie but goodie; smell—smell flowers, grass, trees, a piece of paper, or whatever is around you; touch—put your palms together and rub your hands together fast, feel the friction, and then stop and feel the vibrations in your hands; taste—eat a peppermint or drink peppermint tea as it is known to be calming.

OPPOSITE ACTION

Opposite action is a strategy that helps to regulate our emotions. Increasing our awareness of what we are feeling and where we are feeling it in our body enables us to control our emotions. The opposite action strategy is helpful when your feelings don't fit the facts or when your action isn't effective.

SEVEN STEPS TO OPPOSITE ACTION:

1. Acknowledge your feelings. Describe the emotion. Core emotions include fear, anger, sadness, disgust, joy, and excitement.

2. Identify the facts to determine if your reaction was justified. Does your emotion fit the facts? Is there a good reason to regulate or reduce the intensity of this emotion?. For example, if someone punched you in the face, your anger would be justified. The feeling fits the facts. Becoming angry because your server forgot to bring mustard is unjustified. Although frustrating, an angry reaction is too intense; the feeling doesn't fit the infraction.

3. Is the feeling overpowering? Does it drive you to do dangerous or destructive things?

4. Notice your body language and behavior that accompany the emotion. What's your facial expression, your posture? What are you saying, and how are you saying it? What, specifically, do you do in response to the emotion?

5. Identify the opposite action. Opposite action is involving yourself in an activity that will help you feel better. Examples include exercise, developing hobbies or interests, and interacting with people that support you emotionally. Engage in life.

    Examples of opposite action when experiencing emotions:

    Anger: How can you relax your face and body, so it doesn't scream "I'm angry" or "I'm scared"? How can you acknowledge or ignore the situation rather than react? Opposite action is being kind to the person, building empathy, gently avoiding the person, or working on accepting the situation. If you are willing to change how you feel, solve the problem and change it. Take a break. Express your anger rather than acting it out in fuming rage.

Fear: How can you move toward and not away from something that scares you?

Guilt: If your guilt is justified, change your behavior to match your core values of honesty, integrity, and fidelity. Apologize for what you've done. Make a firm commitment not to do it again. If your guilt is not justified, remember you are acting according to your values.

Shame: Seek out people or find a therapist that you feel safe with to practice vulnerability. It helps to talk with people struggling with similar issues that support you and will not shame you further. Many people struggle with shame and can relate to your story and your feelings.

Disgust: When you are feeling disgusted, try feeling curious and interested.

6. Fully commit to opposite action. Set a time frame to work on it. Explore the consequences of acting on your emotions in the past. What are the possibilities that the situation could happen again?

7. Monitor your emotions. Notice how the original feeling may change or evolve. It helps you shift to a more appropriate reaction.

MOVING FORWARD

A hero's journey is more than completing a workbook—it is the work of one's life. You have navigated a journey that many choose not to take. In what we consider to be the darkest time of your life, you have come to your own aid, which is an act of courage. If you choose to remain in your relationship, expect storms and potholes ahead. Building a healthy relationship requires you to stay in reality and to take care of yourself and use the tools you gained along the way. You have everything you need to handle whatever is around the bend.

Our life journey is never "complete." Through your experience, you understand that you cannot shut the door on the deceit, infidelity, and pain caused by your beloved. You are now able, though, to hold the story in a way that doesn't continue to cause you suffering. The story cannot be forgotten but you can build a new story with your partner.

As you move on to the next part of your journey, we offer the wisdom of our experience working with betrayed, traumatized partners:

- Practice the tools gained on this journey often. When in crisis, people don't remember new strategies they learned to cope with a situation, they default to the old strategies even though they didn't help. Build your muscle memory by making calming breath exercises and other self-care tools a daily practice.

- Stay in reality. Review the information you learned about your betrayer's recovery so that your expectations are realistic.

- Commit to continuing to do the check-in. It is an important tool to restore trust and heal the relationship.

- Remain attuned to your body. When something is amiss, you will feel it in your body first. Catching the anxiety early allows you to use your calming tools so that when you bring up the issue with your betrayer, you will be able to respond to the situation rather than react.

- Review and update your boundaries based on today. The strict boundaries that were created when you were in crisis were set in place to keep you safe; they will not allow a healthy relationship to flourish.

- Keep your anger in check. Use the release exercises to restore inner balance. *There is no health in holding on to anger.*

- Forgiveness is a daily practice.

Continue to work on your story. Review your story and rewrite it as you gain more wisdom. We wish you freedom from the prison of betrayal trauma so that your authentic self can reclaim peace, joy, curiosity, and spontaneity. We wish for you to live the life that you want.

REFERENCES

Chapter 1

Carnes, P.J. (2015). Facing the shadow. Carefree, AZ: Gentle Path Press

Levine, P.A. (1997), Waking the tiger. Berkeley, CA: North Atlantic Books

Cognitive Behaviour Therapy Resources. Emergency or Soothe Box.
http://www.get.gg

Zelano, C., Jiang, H., Zhou, G., Arora, N., Schuele, S., Rosenow, J., Gotfrriend, J.A.
(2016). Nasal respiration entrains human limbic oscillations and modulates
cognitive function. *Journal of Neuroscience.* https://doi.org/10.1523/
JNEUROSCI.2586-16.2016

Chapter 2

Gottlieb, Lori. (2017). I love my girlfriend, why do I keep cheating on her?
New York Magazine

Carnes, P.J. (1989). Contrary to love: Helping the sexual addict. Center City, MN:
Hazelden Publishing

Carnes, P.J. (1991). Don't call it love: Recovering from sexual addiction. Phoenix, AZ:
Gentle Path Press

Hatch, L. (2014). Can serial cheaters change? from http://PsychCentral.com

Dr. Stephanie Sarkis. (2018). Gaslighting: Recognize manipulative and emotionally
abusive people and break free. New York, NY: DeCapo Press

Perel, E. (2018). The state of affairs: Rethinking Infidelity. New York, NY: Harper Paperbacks

Victor, E.C., Sansosti, A.A., Bowman, H.C., Hariri, A.R. (2015). Differential patterns of amygdala and ventral striatum activation predict gender-specific changes in sexual risk behavior. *Journal of Neuroscience.* https://doi.org/10.1523/ JNEUROSCI.0737-15.2015

Cooper, A., Putnam, D.E., Planchon, L.A., Boles, S.C. (2004). Online sexual compulsivity: Getting tangled in the net. *Journal of Sex Addiction and Compulsivity*

Journal of Sex Addiction and Compulsivity, 2007. Online sexual compulsivity: Getting tangled in the net

The Editors of Pediatric Child Health. (2003), Impact of media use on children and youth. 8(5): 301–306.doi: 10.1093/pch/8.5.301

The Editors of Fight the New Drug. (2017). The naked truth: Porn is harmful, and we need to talk about it. https://fightthenewdrug.org

Chapter 3

Diagnostic and statistical manual of mental disorders: Fifth edition. (2013). Washington, DC: American Psychiatric Association

Mate. G. (2010). In the realm of hungry ghosts: Close encounters with addiction. Berkeley, Ca: North Atlantic Books

Bowlby, J. (1983). Attachment and loss. New York, NY: Basic Books

Glass. S. (2007). Not just friends: rebuilding trust and recovering your sanity after infidelity. New York, NY: Free Press

Lindsay, H. (1970). Late great planet earth. Grand Rapids, MI: Zondervan Publishing

Frankel, V.E. (1946). Man's search for meaning. Boston, MA: Beacon Press

Leedes, R., (2001) *Journal of Sexual Addiction and Compulsivity.*

Felitti, V.J., Anda, R.F., Nordenbert, D., Edwards, V., Koss, M.P., Marks, J.S. (1998). Relationship of childhood abuse and household dysfunction to many of the leading causes of death in adults. DOI: https://doi.org/10.1016/S0749-3797(98)00017-8

Chapter 4

Corley, M.D. Schneider, J.P. (2012). Disclosing secrets: An addict's guide for when, to whom, and how much to reveal. North Charleston, SC: Createspace Independent Publishing Platform

Campbell, J. (1990). The hero's journey. New York, NY: HarperCollins

Chapter 5

Brach, T. (2017). Radical acceptance. New York, NY: Bantam Dell.

Gordon, J. The Center for Mind Body Medicine. www.cmbm.org

Pennebaker, J.W. (2004). Writing to heal: A guided journal for recovering from trauma. Oakland, CA: New Harbinger Press.

Vivyan. C. APPLE acronym at www.getselfhelp.co.uk

Chapter 6

Harvard Medical School. www.health.harvard.edu

Linehan, M. (1993). DBT skills training manual, second edition. New York, NY: The Guilford Press

Boszormenyi-Nagy, I. (1987). Contextual family therapy. New York, NY: Springer

Weiss, R. (2017). Out of the doghouse. Deerfield Beach, FL: Health Communications, Inc.

Greenspan, M. (2004). Healing through the dark emotions. Boston, MA: Shambhala Publications, Inc.

Chapter 7

Tutu. D., Tutu. M. (2013). The Book of forgiving: The fourfold path for healing. New York, NY: HarperOne

Wiesel. E. (1958). Night. New York, NY: Hill and Wang

Chapter 10

Johnson, S. (2008). Hold me tight. New York, NY: Little, Brown and Company

Chapter 12

Linehan, M.M. (1993). Skills training manual for treating borderline personality disorder, New York: Guilford Press.

Carnes, P.J. (1993). A Gentle Path through the 12-steps. Center City, MN: Hazelden

McKay, M., Wood, J.C., Brantley, J. (2007). The dialectical behavior therapy skills workbook. Oakland, CA: New Harbinger Publications, Inc.

APPENDIX

Codependents Anonymous. Dallas, TX

Hayes, S. C., Strosahl, K. D., & Wilson, K. G. (1999). Acceptance and commitment therapy: An experiential approach to behavior change. New York, NY: Guilford.

Vivyan, C. Color Breathing at getselfhelp.co.uk

APPENDIX

TRAUMA TOOLKIT: TOOLS FOR COMMON SYMPTOMS OF POST-TRAUMATIC STRESS

FLASHBACKS

For *flashbacks*, which are spontaneous, unwelcome images, thoughts or memories related to your crisis.

Tools: Unhelpful Thought Box, Wise Mind exercise, breathing exercises.

ANXIETY

For *anxiety*, which often makes us feel very detached, dissociated, or unreal. When we get scared, we breathe too quickly and shallowly and our body begins to panic because we're not getting enough oxygen. This causes dizziness, shakiness and more panic. Breathing slower and deeper will stop the panic.

Tools: Safe place visualization, Wise mind exercise, SUDS scale, Breath breaks, Affirmations list, self-talk "everything is okay now. There is no danger. I will get through this."

DETACHMENT

For *detachment*, which feels like numbness, a sense that you are outside of your body looking in, spacey, etc.

Tools: Rub your palms together vigorously, take shoes and sox off and feel the sensation of your feet on the ground, put your head in the freezer for a minute, Anchoring, walk, rub your palm stone.

<u>*PANIC*</u>

For *state of panic*, which is the sense that you can't get a hold of yourself.

Tools: Call the National Suicide Prevention Hotline 800–273–8255. It is staffed 24 hours a day with people trained to help in a crisis. You don't have to be suicidal to call the hotline.

Ask yourself: Where am I, right now? What day is it? What year is it? How old am I? Where do I live? Simple questions help reduce inner turmoil.

Use breath breaks.

HELPFUL COPING STRATEGIES

- Mobilize a support system—reach out and connect with others, especially those who may have shared the stressful event.

- Talk about the traumatic experience with empathic listeners.

- Cry.

- Exercise.

- Relaxation exercise like yoga, stretching, massage; listening to relaxing guided imagery; progressive deep muscle relaxation.

- Humor.

- Prayer and/or meditation.

- Hot baths.

- Music and art.

- Maintain balanced diet and sleep cycle as much as possible.

- Avoid over-using stimulants like caffeine, sugar, or nicotine.

- Commitment to something personally meaningful and important every day.

- Hug those you love, pets included.

- Eat warm turkey, boiled onions, baked potatoes, cream-based soups—these are tryptophan activators, which help you feel tired but good (like after Thanksgiving dinner).

- Proactive responses toward personal and community safety—organize or do something socially active.

- Write about your experience in detail, just for yourself or to share with others.

- Download apps for your smartphone including *Headspace, Calm, Calm Down Now, Inspirations, Lumosity, Simply Being, Insight Timer.*

- Listen to podcasts: *Betrayal Recovery Radio, Sex Help with Carol the Coach, Beyond Bitchy, Helping Couples Heal*

- Use Your Senses to Relax

   - *Vision*: Look at old magazines and choose a picture which reminds you of your safe place; an imaginary spot, like a river, mountain, lake, beach, or meadow, where you could simply relax with no cares in the world and appreciate the wonders of nature.

   - *Hearing*: Create a playlist of your favorite songs and listen when you need a break.

   - *Smell*: Place scented oils or scented candles in the box.

   - *Taste*: Enjoy your favorite ice cream, a small piece of chocolate, a piece of candy, or a stick of gum.

   - *Touch*: Hug a teddy bear (It really works!)

AFFIRMATIONS

Affirmations are a front-line resource to combat negative self-talk, criticism, judgement, guilt and other negative beliefs.

The following is a list of affirmations. Choose those that define how you want to be in the future. If you write your own, use a statement that starts with "I" and use the present tense. See the examples below. Choose one, adapt one, or make up your own. *Affirmations are declarations of what you want to believe to be true about yourself.*

- I am strong...

- I am determined and successful.

- I am a worthwhile person.

- I am a unique and special person.

- I have inner strength and resources.

- I am confident and competent.

- I hold my head up high.

- People like me—I am a likeable person and I like myself.

- I care about others, I am needed and worthwhile.

- I am a loving person.

- I have a lot to be proud of.

- I have all that I need.

- I am in control of my life.

- I can achieve anything I want to achieve.

- I make wise decisions based on what I know.

- I have set my goals and am moving towards them.

- I accept myself as a unique and worthwhile person.

- My life has meaning and purpose.

- I am in control of my choices.

- I am strong and healthy.

- I am calm and confident.

- I have many options and can make wise decisions.

- Everything is getting better every day.

- I am calm and relaxed.

- I am healthy and have all that I need.

- Today is the first day of the rest of my life and I will take notice of the many positive

- things this day has to offer.

- I live a healthy and positive lifestyle.

- I know I can master anything if I practice it continually.

- I can seek inner guidance whenever I need to.

- My life purpose can be whatever I choose it to be.

- All is well, right here, right now.

- I have compassion for myself and for others.

- I am happy living my life.

- I am a worthwhile person, exactly as God intended me to be.

- I am finding my integrity one day at a time.

- I am worthy of love and acceptance, exactly as I am.

- Today, I choose to live in the moment.

- My past actions do not define me in the present.

- I am able to give and receive love.

- I respect the boundaries of others.

- I am recovering with the help of others.

- I have done bad things, but I am not a bad person.

- It is OK for me to talk to others about what I am thinking and feeling.

- I am letting go of my shame.

- I am fully present today.

- I can heal and forgive myself for the harms I have caused.

- I am a better person today than I was yesterday.

- I am able to ask for and accept help when I need it, without feeling ashamed.

- day at a time.

- I am striving for progress, not perfection.

- I am living a better life today than yesterday.

- I am making positive changes in my life, one step at a time.

- Today, my heart is clean.

- I am fearlessly and rigorously honest in all aspects of life.

- Outward failures are learning opportunities. They no longer dishearten me.

- I am living a life of integrity.

- Today, I am living my values.

- Negative feelings are just feelings. They don't last.

- I honor who I am.

- I am worth loving. There is love all around me.

- I am recovering and healing, one day at a time.

- I am enough.

- I am the right person, in the right place, at the right time.

- Today, I choose to be myself, and to be happy with who I am.

- I believe in myself and my abilities.

- Today, I will do small things with great love.

- My sobriety is a journey, not a destination. Today I will enjoy the journey.

- My recovery works when I work it.

- I am worth the effort of recovery.

- I am responsible for the effort, not the outcome.

- Today, I am stronger than my addiction.

- I like myself.

- Happiness is within me.

- My life belongs to me, not my addiction.

- I appreciate and cherish the true me more and more each day.

- I am a happy, peaceful person.

- I am a strong person with healthy habits.

- I am capable of healthy relationships with others.

- My spirit is healing.

- Today, I am walking the right path.

- I am living as God intended.

- All of my problems have a solution.

- I am proud of myself.

- I deserve to be sober and to heal.

- I can and I will.

- Today, I have a choice. And the choice I make is sobriety.

- When troubled, I can stop, breathe, and reach out for help.

- I deserve to be sober and to heal.

- I can and I will.

- Today, I have a choice. And the choice I make is sobriety.

- I can love myself and accept my past.

- When troubled, I can stop, breathe, and reach out for help.

MY BASIC RIGHTS[12]

- I have the right to be treated with respect and dignity.

- I have the right to feel and express my anger responsibly.

- I have the right to honor all my feelings.

- I have the right to expect full honesty in my relationship.

- I have the right to have proof that I am safe from STD infection in my relationship.

- I have the right to follow my own values and standards for myself.

- I have the right to have my needs and wants respected by others.

- I have the right to have my needs be as important as the needs of others.

- I have the right to ask for help; doing everything by myself is not mandatory!

- I have the right to ask why or why not.

- I have the right to say no and not feel guilty.

- I have the right to be in a non-abusive environment.

- I have the right to determine my own priorities.

- I have the right to leave my relationship if my safety or wellbeing are compromised.

- I have the right to a fulfilling sex life.

- I have the right to physical affection in my relationship.

- I have the right to decide how long I stay invested in my relationship if change isn't happening.

---

[12]Adapted from *Codependents Anonymous*

- I have the right to take as long as I need to grieve. I am no longer going to allow you to speak to me in a demeaning manner.

- I have the right to be spoken to without judgment and shame.

- I have the right to choose to discuss my personal struggles with food, spending, mental health.

- I have the right to choose whether to discuss the past.

- I have the right to be seen for exactly who I am.

- I have the right to privacy.

USING MINDFULNESS TO COPE WITH NEGATIVE EXPERIENCES (THOUGHTS, FEELINGS, EVENTS)

With mindfulness, even the most disturbing sensations, feelings, thoughts, and experiences can be viewed from a wider perspective as passing events in the mind, rather than as "us," or as being necessarily true (Brantley 2003).

"When we are more practiced in using mindfulness, we can use it even in times of intense distress, by becoming mindful of the actual experience as an observer, using mindful breathing and focussing our attention on the breathing, listening to the distressing thoughts mindfully, recognizing them as merely thoughts, breathing with them, allowing them to happen without believing them or arguing with them. If thoughts are too strong or loud, then we can move our attention to our breath, the body, or to sounds around us.

"Think of your mind as the surface of a lake or an ocean. There are always waves on the water, sometimes big, sometimes small, sometimes almost imperceptible. The water's waves are churned up by winds, which come and go and vary in direction and intensity, just as do the winds of stress and change in our lives, which stir up *waves in our mind. It's possible to find shelter from much of the wind that agitates the mind. Whatever we might do to prevent them, the winds of life and of the mind will blow."*

~ Jon Kabat-Zinn

QUESTIONING YOURSELF OUT OF DISTRESS

- What am I reacting to?

- What is it that's really pushing my buttons here?

- What is it that I think is going to happen here?

- What's the worst (and best) that could happen?

- What's most likely to happen?

- Is this fact or opinion?

- Am I getting things out of proportion?

- How important is this really? How important will it be in 6 months time?

- What harm has actually been done?

- Am I expecting something from this person or situation that is unrealistic?

- Am I overestimating the danger?

- Am I underestimating my ability to cope?

- Am I using that negative filter? Those gloomy specs? Is there another way of looking at it?

- What advice would I give to someone else in this situation?

- Am I spending time ruminating about the past or worrying about the future? What could I do right now that would help me feel better?

- Am I putting more pressure on myself, setting up expectations of myself that are almost impossible? What would be more realistic?

- Am I mind-reading what others might be thinking?

- Am I believing I can predict the future?

- Is there another way of looking at this?

- What advice would I give someone else in this situation?

- Am I putting more pressure on myself?

- Just because I *feel* bad, doesn't mean things really *are* bad.

- Am I jumping to conclusions about what this person meant?

- Am I mis-reading between the lines?

- Is it possible that they didn't mean that?

- Am I exaggerating the good aspects of others, and putting myself down? Or am I exaggerating the negative and minimizing the positives? How would someone else see it? What's the bigger picture?

- Things aren't either totally white or totally black—there are shades of grey. Where is this on the spectrum?

- This is just a reminder of the past. That was then, and this is now. Even though this memory makes me *feel* upset, it's not *actually* happening again right now.

- What do I want or need from this person or situation? What do they want or need from me? Is there a compromise?

- What would be the consequences of responding the way I usually do?

- Is there another way of dealing with this?

- What would be the most helpful and effective action to take? (*for me, for the situation, and for the other person*)

COLOR BREATHING[13]

From the feelings list, choose the color relating to what you feel you need.

Make yourself comfortable whether sitting or lying.

Close your eyes, and bring your attention to your breathing.

Anytime that other thoughts, images, sounds or sensations come to mind, just notice them, and then gently bring your attention back to your breathing, and your color.

Perhaps imagine that you have a balloon in your belly, and notice how the balloon inflates as you breathe in, and deflates as you breathe out. Notice the sensations in your abdomen as your belly rises as the balloon inflates on the in-breath, and falls as the balloon deflates on the out-breath and mind.

Notice how the color is affecting your body, and your mind, as you allow it to.

Now visualize your color, perhaps in the form of light, or mist. If it's difficult to visualize that color, just imagine, in your mind's eye, something that is that color like green grass, blue sea or sky, orange sunset, pink dawn. See it in front of you, over you, surrounding you, enveloping you. As you slowly breathe become aware of breathing in your color, into your nose, your throat, your chest and abdomen. Imagine now that color spreading out within you, into every part of your body, and notice the effects that it has.

Notice the sensations in your body, as this colored light or mist, flows into and spreads throughout your body gently flow and infuse your body and mind.

Continue to notice the color and the sensations that it brings.

Anytime that your attention wanders, simply notice that it's wandered, then gently bring your focus back to your color.

---

[13]getselfhelp.co.uk

Whenever you're ready, start to bring your attention back to the here and now, where you are. Open your eyes and look around, noticing what you see and what you hear. Take a couple of breaths and notice the pleasing sensations that accompany this relaxing colored breathing.

<u>COLOR</u>

- Breathe in **red** for energy and vitality, strength and will-power.

- Breathe in **orange** for joy, happiness and fun.

- Breathe in **yellow** to increase your objectivity and intellectual abilities.

- Breathe in **green** to cleanse, feel more balanced and to combat tumors.

- Breathe in **turquoise** to boost the immune system, reduce inflammation.

- Breathe in **blue** for relaxation, peace and good sleep.

- Breathe in **violet** for self-respect, dignity and beauty.

- Breathe in **magenta** to let go of obsessional thoughts, images, memories.

Emotions are normal and everyone experiences them. Sometimes, particularly when we have had persistent distressing experiences during our lives, we can emotionally react more often to situations (that others may not find distressing) where we feel threatened. The distress can be very intense and it's difficult to manage ourselves and situations when things are feeling so overwhelming.

Learning Emotion Regulation skills will help us learn to effectively manage and change the way we feel and cope with situations.

Emotions, thoughts and what we do or feel an urge to do (behaviors) are all linked and become vicious cycles. Changing one part of the cycle will help improve the situation and help you feel better.

THE BALCONY VIEW

When something is distressing us, we are often so close to the situation that it is really hard to understand our situation in any other way—because we are in it.

Using a theatre analogy, when we are seated in the orchestra, front row and center, we are immersed in what is happening in the moment between the actors in front of us. We don't even realize the villain is about to enter the scene. The balcony view is very different. From the balcony, you can see the big picture; you can see the flow of the play as a whole and can even predict what will happen next.

Being further from the action has the advantage of perspective. From front row and center, you are a part of the scene. You laugh, cry, get angry. The balcony view is detached. You are able to appreciate the depth and subtleties of the situation without being in it.

The balcony view provides:

- Perspective: the ability to see both sides of the situation.

- Self–Awareness: With distance, emotions cool down and we are able to see how we contributed to the distressing situation (Unless we are the victim, of course)

- Access to the Wise Mind: Perspective allows you to see the situation more clearly. You are able to list the feelings/emotion mind and the Facts/Thinking mind. Self–awareness brings humility, compassion and calm. The wise mind is able to offer guidance and clarity.

METAPHORS

Metaphors help us make sense of complex or sensitive situations. By offering us a structure for how to think, they point us towards what the problem is, and therefore what the solution should be. Metaphors create meaning, enabling us to make sense of circumstances outside of our normal experience.

They help us to see alternative ways of looking at something. Every culture and religion use these types of stories, analogies, and parables to improve understanding, make a point more memorable, and help us make positive changes.

Metaphors help us see thoughts—their nature and role—in a different light. Just that alone, seeing thoughts differently, helps to create a space and a distance between us and our thoughts, which helps us to stand back a little, see things a bit more objectively, and make wiser and more helpful decisions about how to react effectively.

PASSENGERS ON THE BUS

You are the driver of your bus. the passengers (thoughts) are being critical, abusive, intrusive, distracting, and shouting directions, or sometimes just plain nonsense. They may want to jump into the drivers' seat, but if they do, they will take you down a dark road. Tell them to quiet down so you can focus on the road ahead.

THE BEACH BALL

We try to stop thoughts, but that's impossible. It's like trying to constantly hold an enormous inflatable beach ball under the water, that it keeps popping up in front of our faces. We can allow the ball to float around us, just letting it be. So rather than stop the thoughts, we can stop fighting them, and let them be, without reacting to them. (Vivyan 2009)

THOUGHT TRAIN

We can sit on the train, watching the scenery (thoughts, images, sensations) go by, or stand on the platform watching the thought train pass by—we don't have to jump on it.

THE RIVER

Sometimes it feels like we're being carried away downstream, struggling to stay afloat amongst all the mud, filth and debris. That muck and debris are thoughts, sensations, events, feelings, and that river is our distress as we drift helplessly downstream. But we can stand on the riverbank, watching as those thoughts, events, sensations, feelings go by. You might watch individual items as they pass—perhaps a thought floating on a leaf, a sensation as a log, event as on old bicycle.
We can stand and watch.

THE TUNNEL

When we get anxious driving through a tunnel, the best option is to keep going rather than try to escape. This feeling will pass—there is an end to this tunnel.

THE MOUNTAIN

Whatever the weather, or whatever happens on the surface of the mountain—the mountain stands firm, strong, grounded, permanent. We can be like that mountain, observing thoughts, feelings, sensations, knowing inner stillness.

BAD WOLF, GOOD WOLF

Think of the bad wolf and the good wolf as opposite thinking. Distressing thoughts are the bad wolf. They are upsetting, painful, critical and shaming. They can easily take over and lead to depression. The good wolf is compassionate, kind, loyal, courageous, proud, fair, and fiercely protects their pack.

The wolf we feed becomes stronger and stronger.

THE POISONED PARROT

Imagine you're given a parrot. This parrot is just a parrot—it doesn't have any knowledge, wisdom or insight. It's bird-brained after all. It recites things 'parrot fashion'—without any understanding or comprehension. It's a parrot.

However, this particular parrot has been specifically trained to be unhelpful to you—to continually comment on you and your life, in a way that constantly puts you down, criticizing you. For example, the bus gets stuck in a traffic jam, and you arrive at work 5 minutes late. The parrot sits there saying: "There you go again. Late. You just can't manage to get there on time can you. So stupid. If you'd left the house and got the earlier bus you'd have arrived with loads of time to spare and the boss would be happy. But you? No way. Just can't do it. Useless. Waste of space. Absolutely pathetic!"

How long would you put up with this abuse before throwing a towel over the cage or getting rid of the parrot? We can often put up with the thoughts from this internal bully for far too long. Notice that 'parrot'—and cover the cage. Eventually it will tire of the towel and fly away. (Vivyan 2009—based on "The Malevolent Parrot," source unknown)

THE QUICKSAND

When we're stuck in quicksand, the immediate impulse is to struggle and fight to get out. But that's exactly what you mustn't do in quicksand—because as you put weight down on one part of your body (your foot), it goes deeper. So the more you struggle, the deeper you sink—and the more you struggle. Very much a no-win situation. With quicksand, there's only one option for survival. Spread the weight of your body over a large surface area—lay down. It goes against all our instincts to lay down and really be with the quicksand, but that's exactly what we have to do. And so it is with distress. We struggle and fight against it, but we've perhaps never considered just letting it be, and being with the distressing thoughts and feelings, but if we did, we'd find that we get through it and survive—more effectively than if we'd fought and struggled. (Hayes et al. 1999)

THE TRAFFIC ACCIDENT

When there's a traffic accident, police ask for witnesses to come forward and describe what happened. They like to have as many witness statements as possible so that they can build up enough evidence to give them a broader, more realistic version of events. In a traffic accident, there will be many different perspectives on what happened. The driver of one car will have one view, another driver or a passenger will have yet another view. Each onlooker who witnessed the accident will have a slightly different perspective, depending on where they were, how far they were, how good a view they had, what else was going on, how much danger they felt they were in, how the accident affected them, what the accident means to them. It's the same principle with everything—each situation, event, conversation, means something different to all those involved, and also to those not involved. (Vivyan 2009)

TUG OF WAR WITH A MONSTER

Imagine you're in a tug of war with some huge anxiety (or depression etc.) monster. You've got one end of the rope, and the monster has the other end. In between you, there's a huge bottomless pit. You're pulling backward as hard as you can, but the monster keeps on pulling you closer to the pit. What's the best thing to do in that situation?

Pulling harder comes naturally, but the harder you pull, the harder the monster pulls. You're stuck. What do you need to do?

Dropping the rope means the monster's still there, but you're no longer tied up in a struggle with it. Now you can do something more useful. (Harris 2009)

A JUDGEMENT FACTORY

Like Santa's toy factory, the judgement factory churns out criticism continually.

A GARDEN

A metaphor for your life, relationships with family and friends can be cultivated like flowers or vegetables. Relationships, like flowers, need regular watering. They need sunshine. Sometimes they need to be pruned. Sometimes you need to weed the garden to allow growth.

A BATTLE

In a battle, you are always either winning or losing. If a battle represents your relationship it is important to remember that if one person wins, it is on the back of the one who has lost.

A MISSION

A goal-driven experience with intention.

A JOURNEY

A journey is a common metaphor for life as it reminds us that the destination is not our only goal. Like with any form of a journey, there are times when the roads are straight and times when they are winding. There are ups and downs and potholes along the way. And there are often wonderful surprises and fun discoveries that you would never have experienced if it wasn't for the route you chose.

A HOUSE

A building is a solid metaphor for life and can be a reminder that a sturdy foundation is needed before building higher. Once you have a firm foundation in place, whatever that means to you, it's easier to confidently add floors and rooms which will stand the test of time and weather.

A ROLLER COASTER

A roller coaster can be a metaphor for the chaos that follows a crisis.

A KALEIDOSCOPE

The metaphor illustrates not just the variety of lights and colors which make up our world, but the beauty in every person and situation. Cultivating an attitude of gratitude by taking the time to see what isn't obvious at a quick glance can be illustrated by this metaphor.

A MOUNTAIN CLIMB

This metaphor illustrates that it often takes hard work, determination, and sometimes sheer endurance to get where we wish to go. Most mountains paths are not directly uphill, but take us down through valleys to get to the next peak. Emotional resilience allows you to follow the trail as it descends before it turns the corner and heads back up again.

A PRISON

A prison can be a metaphor for a life in which you feel out of control. You may feel like you don't have choices and that others have the power. If this is you, it might be helpful to visualize a key to the door by which you can escape to your freedom, and what that might mean in real life.

A CAGE

A metaphor to describe how anger and unforgiveness imprisons our heart.

ONIONS

Peeling back the layers of a situation or person.

ELEVATOR

The crisis sometimes feels like being trapped in an elevator. It goes up and down and you are not even the one pushing the buttons.

STORMS

They are a part of life. They are unpredictable. They bring dark clouds, thunder, lightning, flooding and, sometimes, loss of power. When the storm passes, there is calm.

MAZE

A maze can be confusing. It is easy to lose your way and hit the same dead ends again and again. There is a way out but it is hard to believe when you are in it.

WAR

Crisis can lead to an internal war. Two factions (sometimes more) in battle. We can often be confused about which side we are on or which side is right.

IDENTIFYING FEELINGS

Although we identify what we are feeling in our thinking mind, feelings are a full body experience. First, our mind interprets what we see, think, or hear, then we feel it in our bodies, and, finally our mind identifies the felt sense with a word—a feeling. We start up in our head, go down into our body, and back up to the head. Up, down, then back up. When we ask someone how they feel, we are asking a thinking question and, if the person is struggling with intense emotion, they probably have no idea what they are feeling. In these instances, ask a down question, for example "*What is happening inside right now.*"

PRIMARY EMOTIONS AND SECONDARY EMOTIONS

PRIMARY EMOTIONS	MAD	SAD	AFRAID	CONFUSED	ASHAMED
SECONDARY EMOTIONS	Bothered	Down	Uneasy	Ambivalent	Awkward
	Irritated	Blue	Cautious	Unsettled	Self-Conscious
	Annoyed	Lonely	Tense	Puzzled	Ambushed
	Angry	Disappointed	Distressed	Distracted	Embarrassed
	Irate	Melancholy	Alarmed	Unfocused	Flustered
	Bummed	Depressed	Shocked	Dazed	Regretful
	Furious	Devastated	Frantic	Lost	Belittled
	Ticked Off	Unhappy	Petrified	Baffled	Sorry
	Indignant	Lonely	Panic Stricken	Flustered	Guilty

PRIMARY EMOTIONS	LONELY	EMBARRASSMENT	FEAR	PEACEFUL	JOYFUL
SECONDARY EMOTIONS	Out of Place	Foolish	Afraid	Content	Ecstatic
	Isolated	Awkward	Nervous	Harmonious	Excited
	Invisible	Silly	Shaken	Tranquil	Cheerful
	Ignored	Mortified	Panicky	Secure	Heartened
	Unwanted	Humiliated	Agitated	Connected	Elated
	Rejected	Disgraced	Jumpy	Intimate	Playful
	Abandoned	Disconcerted	Shaken	Accepting	Hopeful
	Lonesome	Sheepish	Threatened	Compassionate	Lighthearted
	Disconnected	Snubbed	Frightened	Empathetic	Expansive
	Cut Off	Mocked	Scared	Still	Happy

SELF-DEFEATING AND NEGATIVE THOUGHTS

- I don't deserve love.
- I am worthless.
- Who would love me if they knew.
- I'm pathetic.
- I am a failure.
- I am helpless.
- I am a fraud.
- Trust no one.
- I am broken.
- I am not like everyone else.
- I am a sucker.

- I am a bad person.
- I am unworthy.
- I am stupid.
- I am ugly.
- I am not going to make it.
- I am unimportant.
- I can't be trusted.
- I am weak.
- I am not safe.
- I don't deserve.
- I am a loser.

SENSATIONS IN BODY

Open	Expansive	Constricted	Numb	Nervous
Tingly	Light-Headed	Stomach Ache	Tight Chest	Warm
Achy	Bubbly	Full	Bloated	Sweating
Spaced Out	Tender	Suffocating	Shudder	Itchy
Wobbly	Quivering	Clammy	Goose Bumps	Electric
Skin Hurts	Dizzy	Unsteady	Shakey	Empty
Disconnected	Numb	Loving	Nausea	Weak
Calm	Agitated	Muscles Sore	Vision Problem	Pounding
Throbbing	Shivering	Queasy	Bilious	Prickly

READINGS AND PRAYERS FOR RELEASE CEREMONIES

Untitled

Lord, make me an instrument of your peace.

Where there is hatred, let me bring love.

Where there is offense, let me bring pardon.

Where there is discord, let me bring union.

Where there is error, let me bring truth.

Where there is doubt, let me bring faith.

Where there is despair, let me bring hope.

Where there is darkness, let me bring your light.

Where there is sadness, let me bring joy.

O Master, let me not seek as much

to be consoled as to console,

to be understood as to understand,

to be loved as to love,

for it is in giving that one receives,

it is in self-forgetting that one finds,

it is in pardoning that one is pardoned,

t is in dying that one is raised to eternal life.

~ Unknown

<u>Psalm 121</u>

A song for ascents. I shall raise my eyes to the mountains, from where will my help come?

My help is from the Lord, the Maker of Heaven and Earth.

He will not allow your foot to falter; your Guardian will not slumber.

Behold the Guardian of Israel will neither slumber nor sleep.

The Lord is your Guardian; the Lord is your shadow; [He is] by your right hand.

By day, the sun will not smite you, nor will the moon at night.

The Lord will guard you from all evil; He will guard your soul.

The Lord will guard your going out and your coming in from now and to eternity.

~ From the *Old Testament*

<u>Great Spirit Prayer</u>

Oh, Great Spirit,

Whose voice I hear in the winds

and whose breath gives life to all the world.

Hear me! I need your strength and wisdom.

Let me walk in beauty, and make my eyes

ever hold the red and purple sunset.

Make my hands respect the things you have made

and my ears sharp to hear your voice.

Make me wise so that I may understand

the things you have taught my people.

Let me learn the lessons you have hidden

in every leaf and rock.

Help me remain calm and strong in the

face of all that comes towards me.

Help me find compassion without

empathy overwhelming me.

I seek strength, not to be greater than my brother,

but to fight my greatest enemy: myself.

Make me always ready to come to you

with clean hands and straight eyes.

So when life fades, as the fading sunset,

my spirit may come to you without shame.

~ Lakota Sioux Chief Yellow Lark, 1887

Lakota Prayer

Wakan Tanka, Great Mystery,

teach me how to trust

my heart,

my mind,

my intuition,

my inner knowing,

the senses of my body,

the blessings of my spirit.

Teach me to trust these things

so that I may enter my Sacred Space

and love beyond my fear,

and thus Walk in Balance

with the passing of each glorious Sun.

~ Lakota Sioux Chief Yellow Lark, 1887

A Chinook Prayer

May all I say and all I think

be in harmony with thee,

God within me,

God beyond me,

maker of the trees.

~ Prayer from the Chinookan Peoples

Three Step Prayer

First Step: Plant your feet firmly on the earth. Using your five senses, give thanks to our Creator God for the countless ways God comes to us through creation—for all the beauty that your eyes see, for all the sounds that your ears ear, for all the scents that you smell, the tastes that you taste, for all that you feel (the sun, wind, rain, snow, warm, or cold). Pray this day that you may be open and attuned to the countless ways that our Creator God comes to us through your senses, through the gifts of creation.

Second Step: Let go of all the pain, struggle, regret, failures, garbage of yesterday—step out of it—leave it behind, brush the dust of it from your feet.

Third Step: With this third and final step, step into the gift of the new day, full of hope, promise, and potential. Give thanks for the gift of this new day, which God has made!

Amen.

~ José Hobday

Psalm 23

The Lord is my shepherd, I shall lack nothing.

He lays me down in green pastures; He leads me beside still waters.

He revives my soul; He directs me in paths of righteousness for the sake of His Name.

Though I walk in the valley of the shadow of death, I will fear no evil, for You are with me; Your rod and Your staff—they will comfort me.

You will prepare a table for me before my enemies; You have anointed my head with oil; my cup is full.

Only goodness and kindness shall follow me all the days of my life, and I shall dwell in the House of the Lord for many long years.

~ A Psalm by David

RESOURCES

BETRAYAL TRAUMA

S. Carnes, *Courageous Love*, (Carefree, AZ: Gentle Path Press, 2020).

C. Black, *Deceived: Facing the Trauma of Sexual Betrayal* (Las Vegas, NV: Central Recovery Press, 2009).

S. Carnes, *Mending A Shattered Heart: A Guide for Partners of Sex Addicts*, second edition (Carefree, AZ: Gentle Path Press Second Edition, 2011).

M. Corcoran, *A House Interrupted: A Wife's Story of Recovering from Her Husband's Sex Addiction* (Carefree, AZ: Gentle Path Press, 2011).

C. Juergensen Sheets and A. Katz, *Help Her Heal: An Empathy Workbook for Sex Addicts to Help Their Partners Heal* (Claremont, CA: Sano Press, LLC, 2019).

J.D. Corley and J. Schneider, *Disclosing Secrets* (Carefree, AZ: Gentle Path Press, 2002).

K. Skinner, *Treating Trauma from Sexual Betrayal: The Essential Tools for Healing* (Lindon, UT: K Skinner Corp., 2017).

D. Ford, *Awakening from the Sexually Addicted Mind: A Guide to Compassionate Recovery* (Claremont, CA: Sano Press, 2019).

V. Palmer, *Moving Beyond Betrayal*, (Las Vegas, NV: Central Recovery Press, 2016).

M. Laaser, *Shattered Vows*, (Grand Rapids, MI: Zondervan, 2008).

V. Palmer, *Moving Beyond Betrayal*, (Las Vegas, NV: Central Recovery Press, 2016).

BOUNDARIES

H. Cloud and J. Townsend, *Boundaries in Marriage* (Grand Rapids, MI: Zondervan, 2002).

A. Katherine, *Boundaries: Where You End and I Begin* (New York, NY: Fireside Books, 1993).

A. Katherine, *Where to Draw the Line: How to Set Healthy Boundaries Every Day* (New York, NY: Fireside Books, 2000).

R. Lerner, *Living in the Comfort Zone: The Gift of Boundaries in Relationships* (Deerfield Beach, FL: HCI, 1995).

C.L. Whitfield, *Boundaries and Relationships: Knowing, Protecting, and Enjoying the Self* (Deerfield Beach, FL: HCI, 1993).

C. Wills-Brandon, *Learning to Say No* (Lincoln, NE: iUniverse, 2000).

A. Wilson Schaff, *Escape From Intimacy* (San Francisco, CA: Harper, 1989).

FORGIVENESS

D. Tutu, M. Tutu, *The Book of Forgiving*, (San Fransisco, CA: Harper One, 2014)

L. Smedes, *Forgive and Forget*, (San Fransisco, CA: Harper One, 2007)

L. Smedes, *The Art of forgiving*, (New York, NY: Ballantine Books, 1997)

K. Neff, *Self-Compassion*, (New York, NY: William Morrow Paperbacks, 2015)

F. Luskin, *Forgive for Good*, (San Fransisco, CA: Harper One, 2003)

B. Flanigan, *Forgiving the Unforgiveable: Overcoming the Bitter Legacy of Intimate Wounds*, (New York, NY: Wiley Publishing, 1994)

TRAUMA

P. Carnes, *The Betrayal Bond; Breaking Free of Exploitive Relationships*, (HCI, 1997)

C. Courtois, *It's Not You, It's What Happened to You: Complex Trauma and Treatment* (Self-published: 2014).

M. Greenspan, *Healing Through the Dark Emotions; The Wisdom of Grief, Fear and Despair* (Shambala, 2003)

J. Crane, The Trauma Heart: *We Are Not Bad People Trying to Be Good, We Are Wounded People Trying to Heal: Stories of Survival, Hope and Healing* (Deerfield Beach, FL: Health Communications, Inc., 2017).

T. Dayton, *Heartwounds* (Deerfield Beach, FL: HCI, 1997).

T. Dayton, *The Soulful Journey of Recovery: A Guide to Healing from a Traumatic Past for ACAS, Codependents, or Those with Adverse Childhood Experiences* (Boca Raton, FL: Health Communications, Inc., 2019).

R. Gartner, *Beyond Betrayal: Taking Charge of Your Life After Boyhood Sexual Abuse*, (Hoboken, NJ: Wiley & sons, 2005).

P. Levine and A. Frederick, *Waking the Tiger: Healing Trauma: The Innate Capacity to Transform Overwhelming Experiences* (Berkeley, CA: North Atlantic Books, 1997).

B. Van der Kolk, *The Body Keeps the Score*, (New York, NY: Viking, 2014)

P. Walker, *Complex PTSD: From Surviving to Thriving* (Contra Costa, CA: Azure Coyote Publishing, 2013).

COUPLES HEALING

A. Katehakis, *Erotic Intelligence: Igniting Hot, Healthy Sex While in Recovery from Sex Addiction* (Deerfield Beach, FL: HCI, 2010).

E. Marlin, *Relationships in Recovery: Healing Strategies for Couples and Families* (San Francisco, CA: Harper, 1990).

T. Real, *The New Rules of Marriage: What You Need to Make Love Work* (New York, NY: Ballantine, 2008).

B. & G Bercaw, *The Couples Guide to Intimacy,* (California Center for Healing, 2010)

J. Gottman, *The Seven Principles for Making Marriage Work* (New York, NY: Harmony, 2015)

L. Hatch, *Relationships in Recovery,* (Toms River, NJ: Pentacle, 2013)

D. Schnarch, *Passionate Marriage: Sex, Love, and Intimacy in Emotionally Committed Relationships* (New York, NY: W.W Norton & co., 1997).

S. Tatkin, *Wired for Love: How Understanding Your Partner's Brain and Attachment Style Can Help You Defuse Conflict and Build a Secure Relationship* (Oakland, CA: New Harbinger Publications, Inc., 2011)

S. Tatkin, *We Do: Saying Yes to a Relationship of Depth, True Connection, and Enduring Love* (Boulder, CO: Sounds True, 2018)

S. Johnson, *Hold Me Tight,* (New York, NY: HGB, 2008)

R. Weiss, *Out of the Dog House*, (Simon & Schuster, New York, NY: 2017).

L. Spring and M. Spring, *After the Affair: Healing the Pain and Rebuilding Trust When a Partner Has Been Unfaithful* (New York, NY: William Morrow, 1997).

M. Weiner-Davis, *Healing from Infidelity: The Divorce Busting Guide to Rebuilding Your Marriage After an Affair* (Woodstock, IL: Michele Weiner-Davis Training Corporation, 2017).

CYBERSEX ADDICTION

P. Carnes, D. Delmonico, and E. Griffin, *In the Shadows of the Net* (Center City, MN: Hazelden, 2001).

R. Weiss and J. Schneider, *Untangling the Web: Sex, Porn, and Fantasy Obsession in the Internet Age* (Carefree, AZ: Gentle Path Press, 2012).

G. Wilson, *Your Brain on Porn: Internet Pornography and the Emerging Science of Addiction* (United Kingdom: Commonwealth Publishing, 2014).

HEALTHY SEXUALITY

A. Katehakis, *Sexual Reflections: A Workbook for Designing and Celebrating Your Sexual Health Plan* (Los Angeles, CA: Center for Healthy Sex, 2018).

A. Katehakis and T. Bliss, *Mirror of Intimacy: Daily Reflections on Emotional and Erotic Intelligence* (Los Angeles, CA: Center for Healthy Sex, 2014).

E. Nagoski, *Come As You Are: The Surprising New Science That Will Transform Your Sex Life* (New York, NY: Simon and Schuster Paperbacks, 2015).

SHAME AND ANGER

J. Bradshaw, *Healing the Shame That Binds You* (Deerfield Beach, FL: HCI, 2005).

B. Brown, *The Gifts of Imperfection: Let Co of Who You Think You're Supposed to Be and Embrace Who You Are* (Center City, MN: Hazelden, 2010).

H. Lerner, *The Dance of Anger: A Woman's Guide to Changing the Patterns of Intimate Relationships* (New York, NY: Harper Collins, 1985).

R. Potter-Efron and P. Potter Efron, *Letting Co of Shame: Understanding How Shame Affects Your Life* (Center City, MN: Hazelden, 1989).

R. Potter-Efron, *Handbook of Anger Management* (New York, NY: Routledge, 2005). B. Shoshanna, *The Anger Diet: Thirty Days to Stress-Free Living* (Kansas City, KS: Andrews McMeel Publishing, 2005).

MEN'S ISSUES

K. Adams, *When He's Married to Mom* (New York, NY: Simon & Schuster, 2007).

K. Adams, *Silently Seduced: When Parents make Children their Partners*, (Boca Raton, FL: Health Communications, Inc., 2011).

R. Fisher, *The Knight in Rusty Armor* (Chatsworth, CA: Wilshire Book Co., 1989).

S. Real, *I Don't Want to Talk About It: Overcoming the Secret Legacy of Male Depression* (New York, NY: Fireside, 1998).

E. VandeReis, *On the Journey: Poems of Betrayal and Hope* (Carefree, AZ: Gentle Path Press, 2018).

RECOVERY AND THE TWELVE STEPS

Anonymous, *Alcoholics Anonymous 4th Edition* (New York, NY: AA World Services, 2001).

Anonymous, *Courage to Change: One Day at a Time in Al-Anon* (New York, NY: Al-Anon Family Group Head Inc., 1992).

Anonymous, *Hope for Today* (New York, NY: Al-Anon Family Group Headquarters, 2007).

Anonymous, *Sex and Love Addicts Anonymous* (San Antonio, TX: The Augusüne Fellowship, 1986)

Anonymous, *Recovering Couples Anonymous Blue Book* (Oakland, CA: Recovering Couples Anonymous, 1996).

SEX ADDICTION

P. Carnes, *Don't Call It Love: Recovery from Sexual Addiction* (Center City, MN: Hazelden, 1992).

P. Carnes, *Out of the Shadows: Understanding Sexual Addiction* (Center City, MN: Hazelden, 2001).

P. Carnes, *Facing the Shadow: Starting Sexual and Relationship Recovery* (Carefree, AZ: Gentle Path Press, 2001).

R. Weiss, *Cruise Control: Understanding Sex Addiction in Gay Men* (Carefree, AZ: Gentle Path Press, 2012).

K. McDaniel, *Ready to Heal*, (Carefree, AZ: Gentle Path Press, 2012)

R. Weiss, *Sex Addiction 101*, (Dublin, OH: Telemachus Press, 2018)

S. Arterburn, *Every Mans' Battle*, (Colorado Springs, CO: WaterBrook, 2020)

A. Susskind, *Its Not About the Sex*, (Las Vegas, NV: Central Recovery Press, 2019)

M. Barta, *Tinsa* (Createspace Independent Publishing, 2017)

R. Weiss, J. Schneider, *Always Turned On* (Carefree, AZ: Gentle Path Press, 2015)

SPIRITUALITY AND DAILY MEDITATION

Anonymous, *The Courage to Change* (New York, NY: Al-Anon Family Group, 1992).

M. Beattie, *Journey to the Heart* (Center City, MN: Hazelden, 1990).

M. Beattie, *The Language of Letting Go* (Center City, MN: Hazelden, 1990).

K. Casey, *Each Day a New Beginning* (Center City, MN: Hazelden, 1982).

P. Coelho & A.R. Clarke, *The Alchemist* (New York, NY: Harper, 2006).

E. Kurtz and S. Ketchum, *The Spirituality of Imperfection* (New York, NY: Bantam, 1993).

E. Larsen, *Days of Healing, Days of Joy* (Center City, MN: Hazelden, 1987).

K. Casey, *Each Day a New Beginning*, (Center City, MN: Hadelden, 1982)

Anonymous, *Touchstones for Sex Addiction* (Center City, MN: Hazelden, 1986)

A. Schaef, *Meditations for Women Who Do Too Much*, (New York, NY: HarperOne, 2004)

FINANCIAL ADDICTION

D. Kaplan, *For Love and Money: Exploring Sexual & Financial Betrayal in Relationship* (Create Space Independent Publishing, 2013)

T, Klontz, et al., *The Financial Wisdom of Ebenezer Scrooge*, (Boca Raton, FL: Health Communications, 2008)

THE BRAIN

L. Brizendine, *The Female Brain* (New York, NY: Three Rivers Press, 2007).

L. Brizendine, *The Male Brain* (New York, NY: Three Rivers Press, 2011).

H. Fisher, *Why We Love: The Nature and Chemistry of Romantic Love* (New York, NY: Henry Holt, 2004).

A. Levine & R. Heller, *Attached: The New Science of Adult Attachment and How it Can Help You Find-and Keep-Love*, (New York, NY. Penguin, 2010).

S. Tatkin, *Wired for Love: How Understanding Your Partner's Brain & Attachment Style Can Help You Defuse Conflict & Build a Secure Relationship* (Oakland, CA: New Harbinger, 2011).

PODCASTS, BLOGS, VIDEOS

PODCASTS:

- *Betrayal Recovery Podcast* by APSATS

- *Beyond Bitchy* with Vicki T. Palmer

- *Love and Sex Today* with Dr. Doug Weiss

- *Sex, Love and Addiction* with Dr. Rob Weiss

- *Helping Couples Heal* Podcast with Duane Osterlind & Marnie Breecker

- *Sex, Love and Relationships* with Carol the Coach

BLOGS:

- www.partnerhope.com

- www.beyondbitchy.com

YOU TUBE VIDEOS:

- Dr. Gabor Mate: *The Power Hour*

- Brené Brown: *Vulnerability and Shame*

- Paula Hall: *Can Couples Survive Sex Addiction*

- Moshe Zev Lamm: *What's Happening inside a good marriage*

- Paula Hall: *Road to Brighton*

- Stan Tatkin : *We Do*

- Dr. Gabor Mate: *How Childhood Trauma Leads to Addiction*

- *Men's and Women's Brains* with Mark Gungor

- The Gottman Institute

- *Your Brain on Porn*, Gary Wilson, TedX

RESOURCES FOR PEOPLE STRUGGLING WITH SEX ADDICTION

- Pure Desire (Christian groups)

- Guard Your Eyes and PA (Porn Anonymous) – 12-Step Recovery for Porn Addicts (p-a.online) (Jewish Online Resources)

- www.intherooms.com

- www.sa.org

- 12-step SLAA (Sex and Love Addicts Anonymous)

- 12-Step SAA (Sex Addicts Anonymous)

- 12-Step ARP (Addiction Recovery Program)

INTERNET BLOCKING SOFTWARE

Blocking software, although helpful, isn't a guarantee sobriety. Many people struggling with sex addiction find the support helpful.

- Covenant Eyes

- Qusstodio Parental Control

- Net Nanny

ABOUT THE AUTHORS

MICHELE F. SAFFIER, LMFT, CSAT-S

Michele F. Saffier has been practicing as a licensed Marriage and Family Therapist since 1993. As Clinical Director and Founder of Michele Saffier & Associates, she and her clinical team have worked with couples, families, betrayed partners, and people in recovery from sexually compulsive behavior for twenty-four years. She has presented lectures on betrayal trauma for the American Association of Sexuality Educators, Counselors and Therapists (AASECT), the International Institute for Trauma and Addiction Therapists (IITAP), the Pennsylvania Association of Marriage and Family Therapists (PAMFT), S-ANON (12-step program for families of people with sexual addiction), among others.

As Co-Founder of The Center for Healing Self and Relationships, she facilitates outpatient treatment intensives for individuals, couples and families healing from the impact of betrayal trauma.

As a master clinician, Michele consults with licensed therapists and colleagues; facilitates trainings and workshops; and creates curriculum for treatment programs. She is available for speaking engagements, trainings, and consultation.

Michele is a Certified Sex Addiction Therapist and Supervisor, Level III Attachment-focused EMDR Practitioner, Level III trained in Gottman Method, Certified Clinical Trauma Practitioner, Certified Adolescent Group Psychotherapist, received advanced training in psychodrama and experiential methods, and is a Level I Internal Family Systems practitioner.

ALLAN J. KATZ, LPC, CSAT

Allan J. Katz, known as the "Healthy Intimacy Coach," helps individuals and couples foster healthy intimacy, improve communication and stop addiction.

Allan is the author of four other books, *Addictive Entrepreneurship Dealing with the 13 Steps to Freedom from Work/Life issues* and *Experiential Group Therapy Interventions with DBT: A 30 Day Program for Treating Addictions and Trauma.* His latest book is, *Hey! What About Me: How to Make Yourself and Others a Priority in a World of Indifference, Impulsivity, and Distraction.* He also co-authored *Help.Her.Heal* by Carol Juergensen Sheets. He is a Licensed Professional Counselor and a Certified Sex Addiction Therapist.

For the past six years, he has worked as a group and individual counselor in a drug and alcohol rehab center in Southaven, Mississippi. He now exclusively counsels private individuals and couples for relationship and intimacy issues, addictions and trauma resolution in Memphis, Tennessee.

Mr. Katz trains other therapists on using experiential therapy methods in group work for treating addictions and trauma and is available to speak at conferences, clubs and meetings.